AF473911

PARALLEL LINES: **EILEEN COOPER**

Royal
Academy
of Arts

Published on the occasion of the exhibition
PARALLEL LINES: EILEEN COOPER AND LEICESTER'S ART COLLECTION
Leicester Museum & Art Gallery, 10 September–27 November 2022

CONTENTS

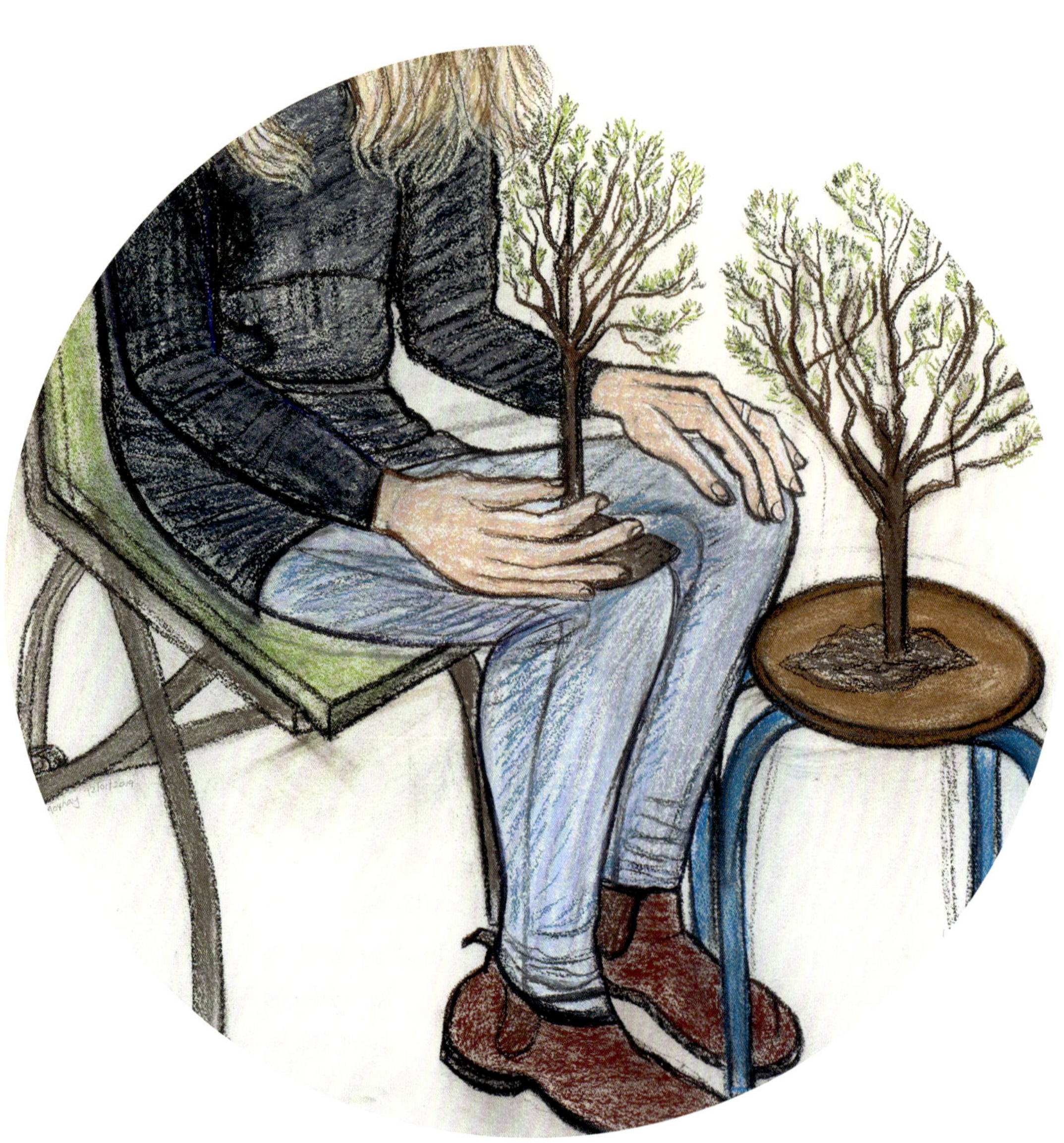

Detail: *Suzanne Moxhay* (p. 68)

PARALLEL LINES
KATHLEEN SORIANO

> ***'Artists learn and develop not only from the past but also through their connections with the present. I have been fortunate enough to benefit from both – an appreciation of what has come before me, as well as a fascination, and a sense of responsibility for what is in the process of becoming.'***
>
> EILEEN COOPER, 2022

Eileen Cooper has been a consistently successful artist across her 50-year career with works entering both public and private collections. Defying those who claimed that it is impossible for a woman to achieve artistic success whilst simultaneously raising children, Cooper has embraced all that motherhood brings, absorbing the characters, the complexity of relationships, emotions, and experiences into her work.

Not unlike Cooper herself, that career trajectory has been solid, measured, evenly paced without the dramas of the highs and lows that some artists encounter as they go in and out of fashion. That quiet balance has however meant that Cooper has not always received the recognition that she deserves, not just for her own work but for the encouragement and development of the work of others through her teaching posts at some of the UK's most important art schools.

In considering Cooper's contribution it is important to reflect on where she has come from and how the artist was formed. Born in Glossop, Cooper first studied art at Ashton-under-Lyne, going on to Goldsmiths and finally the Royal College of Art (RCA). Between 1977 and 2000, while raising her two sons, she taught at a range of art schools across the country including Falmouth, City & Guilds, Camberwell, St Martin's, the RCA and Leicester Polytechnic (as it was then known). Artists can be like magpies,

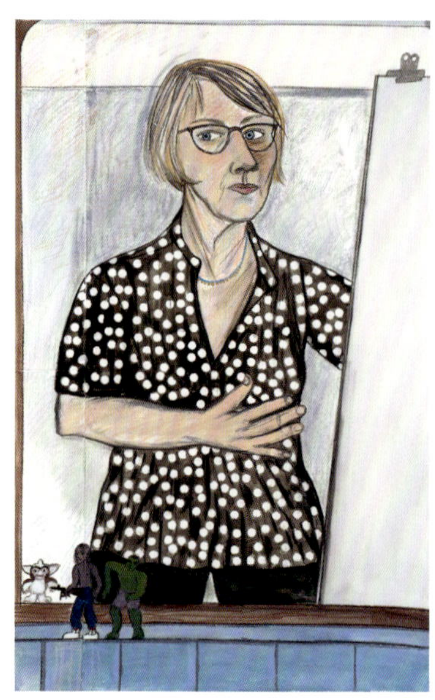

Self-portrait with Toys 2018 (p. 65)

drawing on the physical and cultural world around them for inspiration and creative ideas. Cooper was no different and her work is directly shaped by her experiences and her encounters as well as her physical context, be it at home in the studio, in Lebanon, or out in the Suffolk landscape as with her current body of work.

The exhibition of Eileen Cooper's work at Leicester Museums considers the ways in which artists take their inspiration. It brings together her work from across her career and a selection of related works from Leicester's collections that resonate specifically, thematically or art historically. It considers artistic influence and key themes in art history, as well as how our museum collections have impacted on artists today, examining where ideas and inspiration come from. What are the artistic traditions that artists sit in? Which subjects and genres do they return to? Given Cooper's natural debt to German Expressionist printmaking, a strength of Leicester's collections, and her knowledge of the museums from her time spent teaching in the city, Leicester Museums has provided a natural home for this particular examination of Cooper's work and her approach to making work.

Divided into 10 sections, the exhibition begins with a consideration of Cooper's portraiture from the more recent self-portraits to the double and group portraits that so proliferate in her work. Cooper's figures are always active, in the process of vigorous doing and occasionally mirroring, or responding to each other in their movements, often entangled, contorted, and the hands usually busy – holding, touching, digging. In her double portraits there is often a sense of duality and balance between the two, a symmetry. Where women are paired, the female figure is frequently twinned as if id and ego, two versions of themselves, or of the self even. Cooper has previously commented on her depiction of younger women, referring to them as alternative selves. Her approach serves to draw attention to the way in which Cooper's characters are always tied together in some form of relationship, rarely are they disconnected or acting in isolation.

From her early work to the present day, Cooper's bodies are performative. Apparent from the 1980s, her storytelling facility appears to mine mythology, fables and stories from the Old Testament, although she is more often using imagination and memory as a rich source. Reading a Cooper work challenges the viewer to search for allegory and symbolism. The magic realism tag that is so associated with her painting comes from the often dreamlike quality of her work, the combination of the real and the fantastical, all accentuated by her heightened colourful palette and the often strange geometries that appear in her compositions, contributing to a sense of mood and unease. Geometric forms abound in Cooper's work, often populated by windows, canvasses, mirrors and ladders. It is not unusual

The Two Gardeners 1989 (p. 37)

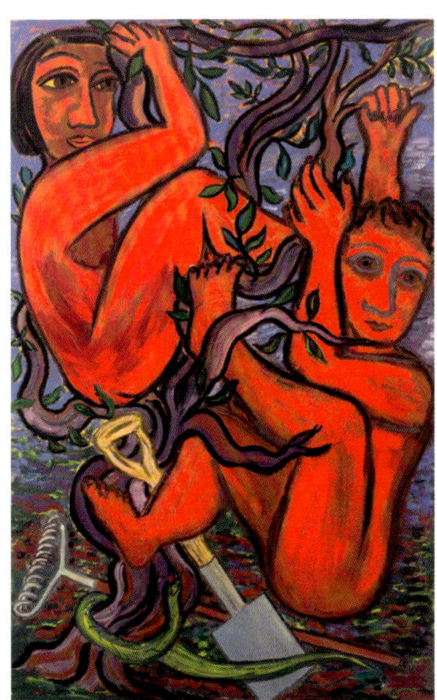

to find paintings within Cooper's paintings, nor for the subject of her work to be the making of the work.

The second section of the exhibition considers Cooper's relationship with modern British art, going on to celebrate her achievements, first as Head of Printmaking and subsequently as Keeper of the Royal Academy (RA) Schools, where she taught from 2010–17. That celebration is achieved through the display of three works from over 50 drawings of her artist students that Cooper has produced since initiating the series in 2018. Cooper's love of teaching, and her ongoing care for her students, is evident through this body of work. Always keen to learn from her students she has taken inspiration from the way in which they move freely between art forms, from traditional painting to digital processes, performance and installation. There is a long tradition of great artists painting each other as a form of homage. Cooper continues that tradition, yet the series is unusual in that it represents a large cohort of artists captured in the very early stages of their careers. In making this body of work she abided by a series of self-imposed rules: using only charcoal, pencils, pastels (occasionally watercolour) on paper, always from life, and largely completing the works in a single sitting of three to four hours.

Drawing has always figured prominently in Cooper's oeuvre. In its large scale she frequently challenges the idea of a

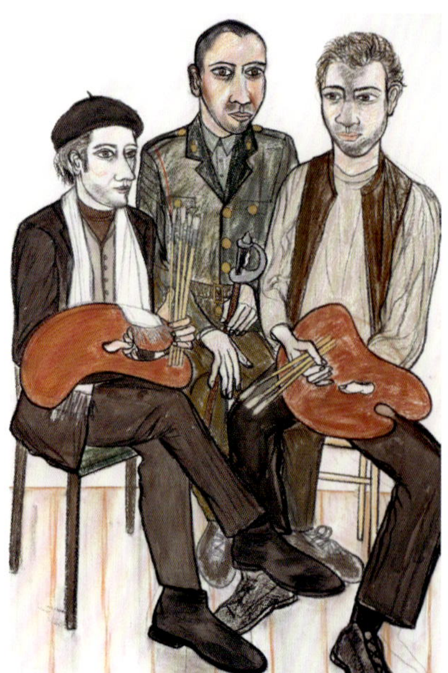

Max Prus, Ziggy Grudzinskas and Joel Wyllie 2019 (p. 63)

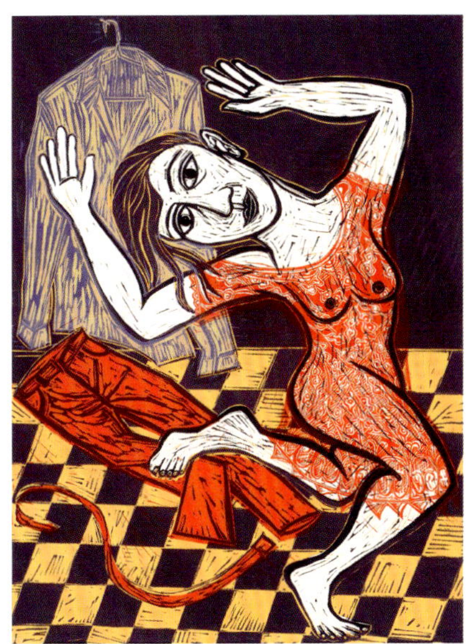

Red Dress 2009 (p. 43)

preparatory study, with the works becoming formidable, finished pieces in themselves. For Cooper it is as much about the materiality of paper and the opportunities that it provides. As well as drawing and printmaking, collage plays an important part in Cooper's dynamic relationship with the support.

The third section of the exhibition in many ways forms the heart of the show with its focus on German Expressionism and printmaking. Cooper states that printmaking has taught her how to think in layers, the collaborative nature of it being distinctively Cooper.

Later sections of the exhibition move to a more thematic consideration focussing on the nude, La Toilette, beasts, dance and circus, as well as a bringing together of ceramics by Cooper with a related collection from Leicester Museums. Each of these groupings highlights key elements and values within Cooper's work, alongside the ongoing interest of artists past and present in these enduring themes.

For Cooper, in nearly all of these sections, the female form dominates, usually in control and most certainly guiding the action. Often simplified in form, her figures burst out of the picture frame, barely contained within the canvas. Occasionally floating or climbing, but nearly always in some form of complex balance – a theme that has been prevalent in Cooper's work, drawing parallels with her life as an artist and a woman, with its burden of sexuality. Softly folding forms, her figures are

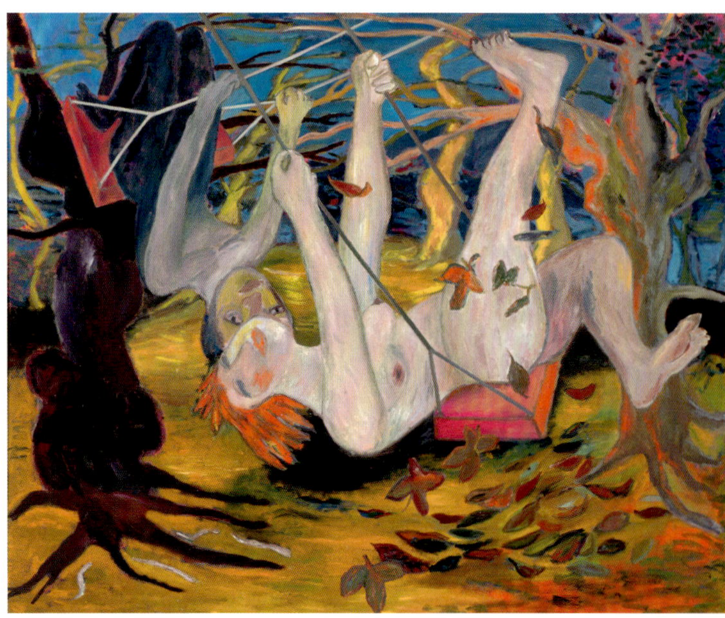

The Swing 1982 (p. 131)

rarely angular (except in her printmaking), and in their nakedness and colour have a sense of being of nature, with a raw sexuality to them.

The human relationship with totemic nature, as she refers to it, is represented powerfully in Cooper's paintings. If they are not populated by creatures, they are filled with plants or her beloved trees. The frequent presence of water in some form or other further alludes to her interest in weightlessness, levitation and fluidity. Whether in the open air, or in the studio, Cooper's iconography is always rich. Surrounded by objects, seemingly loaded with meaning, it takes time to absorb the intention behind Cooper's work. This is not always helped by the titles that she ascribes to the work, each carefully considered and intended by her to add impact to any interpretation.

Inspiration for the artist has also come from the real, not just the imaginary. A long interest in dance was fuelled when Cooper was invited to take up an artist residency at the English National Ballet, during rehearsals for Akram Khan's 2016 production of 'Giselle', which resulted in a new body of work created largely from life. Similarly, Cooper's childhood memories of visiting the circus at Blackpool Tower, and a trip to Moscow where she saw the Moscow State Circus, inform her interest in acrobatics as subject matter. The work becoming, for her, less about the fun of the fair and more about the perils of negotiating the complexities of life and the required need for balance, made even more poignant in her paintings where only a single figure is present – alone in a complicated and dangerous environment.

This publication, aligned with the display of Eileen Cooper's work at Leicester Museums, illustrates fewer collection works than are featured in the exhibition but includes additional works by Cooper associated with the key themes. In so doing, it has provided a rare and welcome opportunity to consider Cooper's oeuvre across her career. This survey approach serves only to highlight the range and variety within her work, demanding an overall reassessment and understanding of her influence and place in contemporary painting. For an artist so closely associated with a specific style of figurative painting it can be difficult to challenge the general perception of their work so that in their artistic consistency they are judged to be repetitive or predictable. This selection of Eileen Cooper's takes us back to some of the earliest work and brings us up to the present day, clearly illustrating her comfort with a wide range of media and styles, her broad range of subject matter, her distinctively female gaze, her strength, conviction, and commitment to making sense of the world around her, around us.

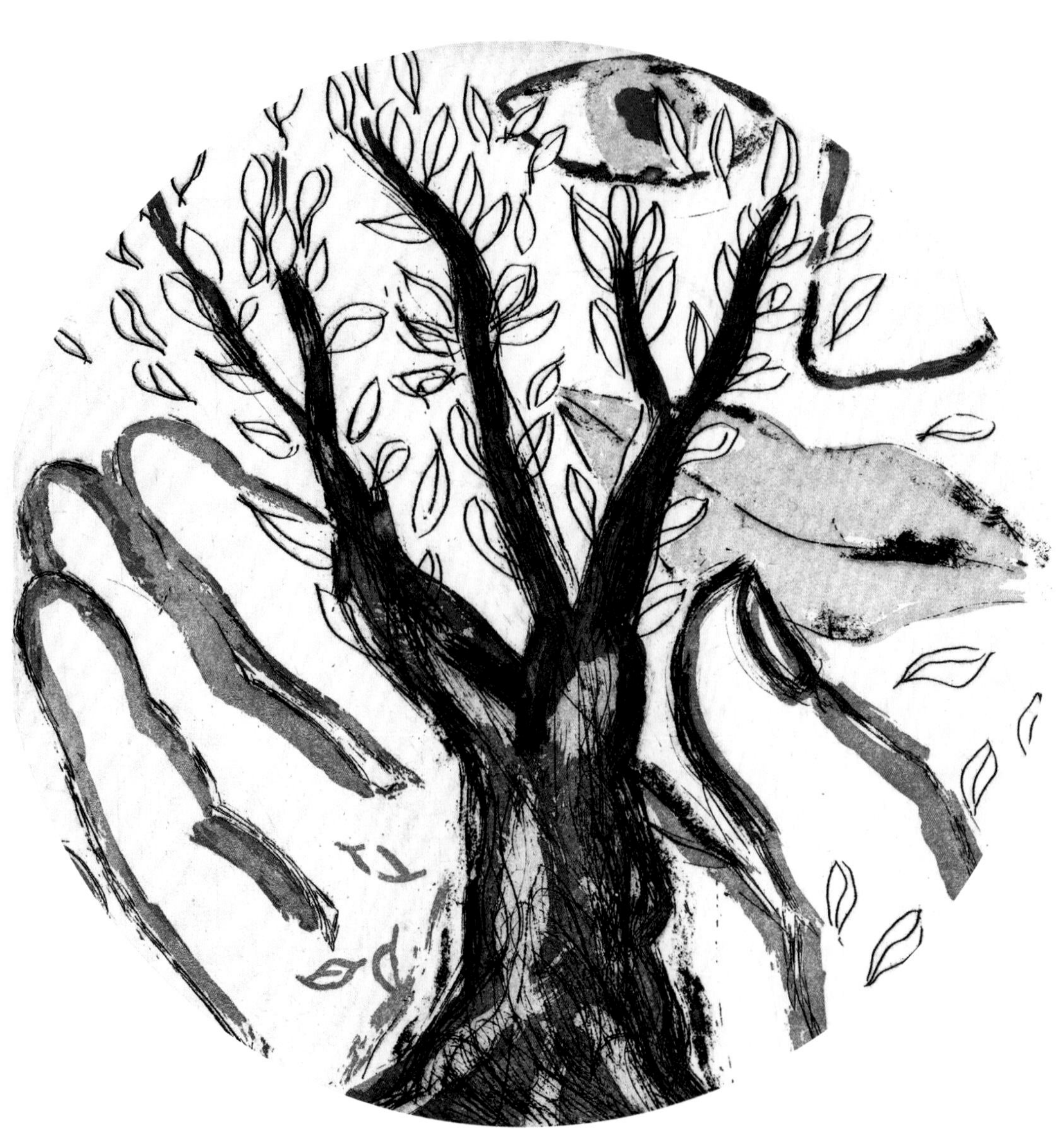

Detail: *Tree of Life* (p. 21)

FROM THE INSIDE OUT
LINSEY YOUNG

> ***To feel deeply, or admit to feeling deeply, is also unadmissible, though not as inadmissible as to admit to having been Un-free.***[1]

Eileen Cooper's work might be said to be about attachment, attachment to the female self, and all its inherent contradictions of loving, caring, creating and bearing. Experiences that have so long been frowned upon because they disrupt the neat patriarchal understandings of women as virgin or whore where never the twain shall meet. There is often an 'unfreeness' in Cooper's women who are so seldom alone, more commonly depicted in their roles as mother, lover or provider. To depict this – within a culture that remains dominated by stories of masculinity, unattached and heroic – continues to be a fearless endeavour.

I met Cooper in 2021 when I was undertaking research around feminist art making in the UK during the 1970s and 1980s. Since then I have been pursuing slow, methodical conversation-based research, adopting what I understand to be a female methodology of paying attention to the everyday, giving space for emotion ('crying is a political act' I was told early on by the artist and feminist Adele Patrick) and attempting to undo the phallocentric arts education I received. My conversation with Cooper, a successful and lauded artist, would prove instrumental in understanding the complexity of negotiations required by a female artist looking to depict her everyday experience, and into understanding the compartments that women artists are placed in, to make their work more palatable to an industry still dominated by men.

Born and brought up in the Peak District 'by a family of shopkeepers', Cooper talks of the powerful matriarchal lineage of sister, mother and grandmother that raised her. Drawing with her mother in biro on whatever paper came to hand, her creative interests were nurtured. She continued to focus on the female experience, rooted in the day-to-day, sexuality, motherhood, home and work. Such thematics have historically been easy to disregard as 'domestic', but with that word being used as a patriarchal slur, it negates, or simply fails to recognise, the passion, fury and commitment that it takes to build and maintain these spaces.

Attending Goldsmiths in 1971 at the age of 18, Cooper landed in London at the beginnings of the Women's Liberation movement in the UK and a year after the first Women's Liberation conference in Oxford. This was a time when many of her female contemporaries were eschewing drawing and painting in favour of performance, conceptual practices, attending consciousness raising groups, and challenging the status quo. While deeply connected to these interests Cooper stayed steadfast to her practice, using charcoal to explore the interiority of the female condition. Cooper's work at this time is highly charged, focusing heavily on questions of the identity and sexuality of a young woman. It is characterised by a rolling sense of movement, naked female bodies climbing and ascending ladders, reflected in mirrors, layered forms that could be a multitude of bodies or one repeated and intertwined – they become emblems for the different ways in which a woman might understand her place in the world. Part of her decision to pursue drawing with such fervour was in part due to a discomfort with the spaces available to women at art school, which were almost always male-led and where the performing female body might be vulnerable to an unsympathetic gaze. Work on paper in this context of the art school in the 1970s and 1980s allowed a degree of privacy and safety within the 'boys club' environment.

The question – *are you a feminist artist?* – was asked often, perhaps because the political content of Cooper's work is implicit rather than explicit. Despite the challenges of this time there was a great deal of community and freedom and the 'generational luck', as she has described it, of affordable housing and materials provided by the college. These conditions all contributed to support Cooper in becoming one of the most highly regarded artists of her year.

Following Goldsmiths, Cooper undertook an MA in painting at the Royal College of Art and describes a 'period of crisis' due to the different challenges of the course but also the continuing discussion, sometimes vitriolic, of male tutors about her work and ambition. Following graduation and a year teaching in Falmouth, she returned to Deptford and took up a studio where, in her words, 'things happened quickly'. She began exhibiting, teaching art to youth and community groups and was soon in post at Leicester Polytechnic. Also, she was now represented by a commercial gallery and numerous solo exhibitions followed.

Cooper's interest in art history is intertwined with a lifelong and deep commitment to non-Western art that she attributes to her Northern roots, hardwired to notice those considered as outsiders. For someone looking beyond the canon, a traditional art school education such as Cooper's would not be without frustrations and on leaving education she began self-led research into the work of women artists such as Frida Kahlo, Alice Neel and Mary Cassatt whose influence resonates in her work to this day.

In 1980 Cooper's work was selected for inclusion in the pivotal exhibition 'Women's Images of Men', organised by the ICA. Part of a trilogy of shows focused on the work of women artists selected by Joyce Agee, Catherine Elwes, Jacqueline Morreau and Pat Whiteread, Cooper exhibited two paintings and a drawing – *Cartwheel*, *Two Figures on a See-saw* and *Figures on Ladder*.

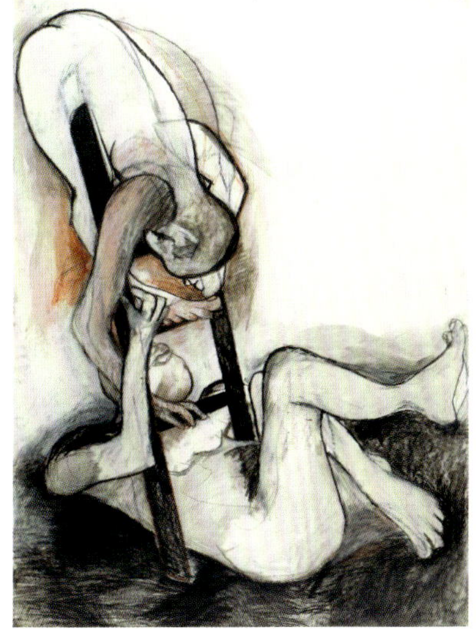

Figures on Ladder 1979
Charcoal on paper, 137 × 101.5 cm
(Not in the exhibition)

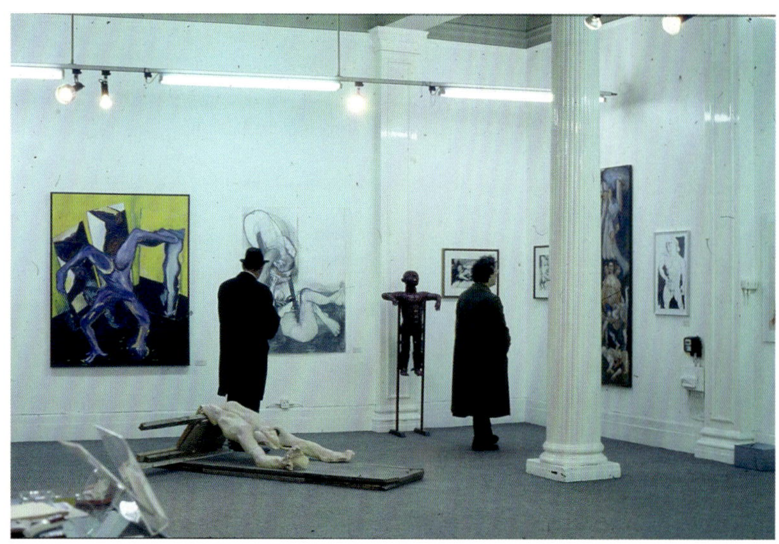

Installation photograph of ICA 'Women's Images of Men' exhibition at The Bluecoat, Liverpool, 1981

An astonishing review of the exhibition by Waldemar Januszczak from *The Guardian* in October 1980 concludes that the work on show is blaming you (men) for absolutely everything[2]. In another review in the *New Statesman* John Spurling states 'these artists strike one as dilettantes, people who don't invest much of themselves in their art. What investment they do make is often a mere parody of or a counterweight to somebody else's conviction'[3]. Quite apart from feeling the need to explain the term dilettantes to its readers, this beautifully demonstrates the disrespect by mainstream culture for the female experience and a profound misunderstanding of the importance and relevance of women's work.

> *In hospital I felt immediately a sort of animal-like habituation with her presence; at home I am in transitional shock, as if I had been out and bought something extremely expensive, something for which in the shop I felt the fiercest most private desire, and were now regarding it with shrivelled courage in my living room ... I both want it and fear it, and yet can consummate neither my desire nor my fear, can neither use nor relinquish this precious purchase for my feelings constrict each other and hold me in a kind of deadlock.*[4]

Cooper gave birth to her first child in 1984 and from that moment her work expanded to include images of her children and activities as a mother. This proved too much for some and she remembers direct criticism from a previously supportive female journalist who now felt this was a disappointment, that somehow acknowledging the experience of motherhood was an act of failure on the part of the artist. Perhaps this relates to the notion of the tortured genius artist that Cooper had long been kicking against or just to the casual misogyny that permeates women's lives; but it had a profound effect on Cooper's career, and an overriding sense that her seemingly positive visualisations of domestic life placed her into a different category of artist, somehow more palatable or decorative.

Whilst there are tender and beautiful portrayals of motherhood in Cooper's work they are never without complexity. *Putting Down Roots*, 1985, made the year after the birth of her first son, is a monumental canvas which, at its centre, features a woman's lower legs, her hands reaching down to touch plants and her feet interconnected with underground roots that grow over the stomach and breasts of a reclining naked female body. Behind the standing woman's legs, a male face and the figure of a baby sit hovering in an abstracted background. This work places the female body at the centre of all life, one that is fertile, grounded and that becomes a planet around which the family orbits. It brings to mind the work of Goddess movement, feminist and painter Monica Sjoo whose *God Giving Birth*, 1968, an image

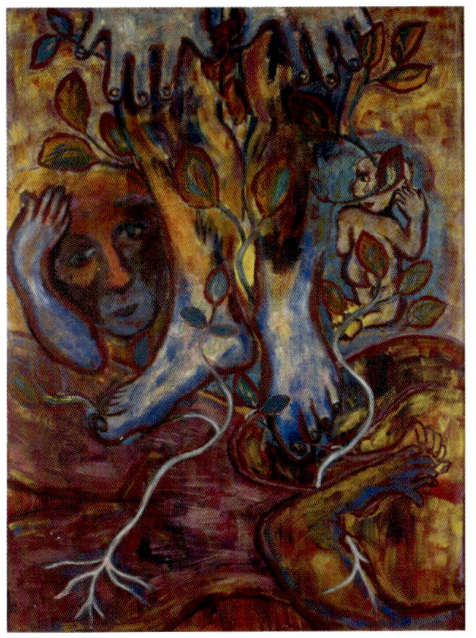

Putting Down Roots 1985
Oil on canvas, 243.3 × 182.2 cm
Arts Council Collection, Southbank Centre, London
(Not in the exhibition)

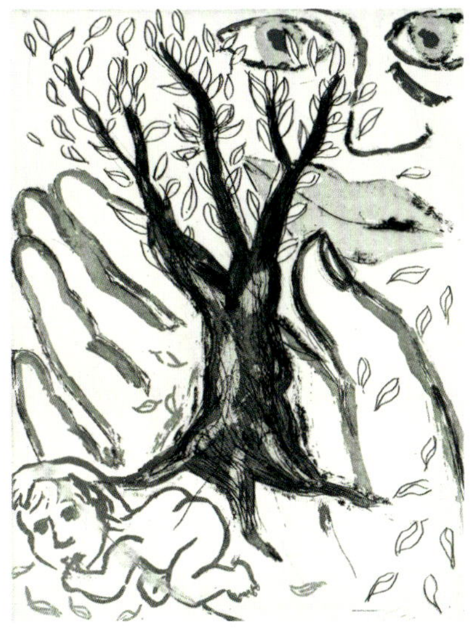

Tree of Life 1986
Etching, 26 × 21 cm (57 × 38 cm)
(Not in the exhibition)

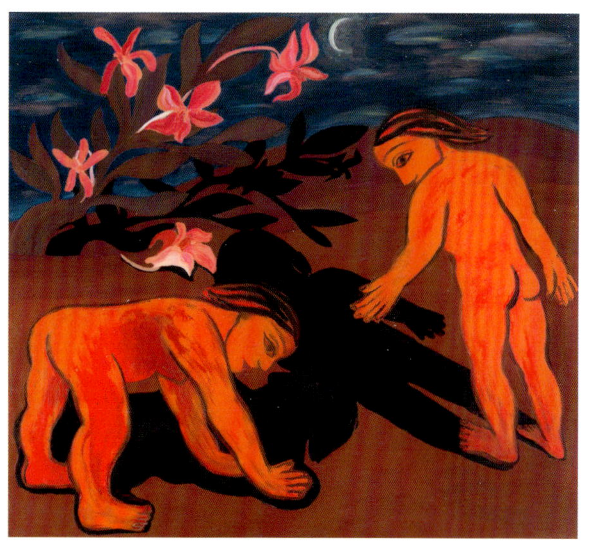

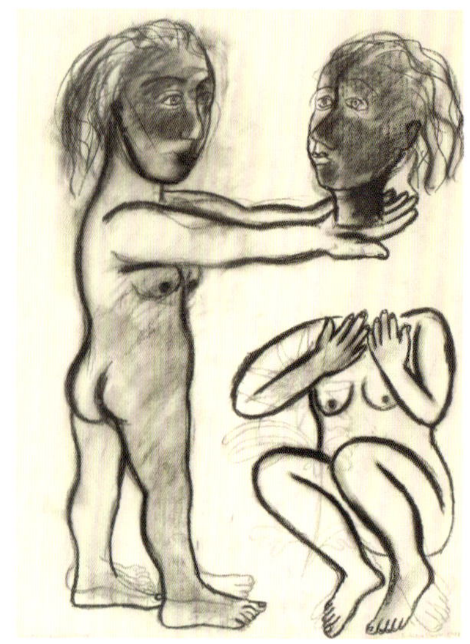

Woman Examining Her Shadow
1989–90
Oil on canvas, 152.5 × 167.5 cm
(Not in the exhibition)

Woman Rebuilding Herself I 1991
Charcoal on paper, 66 × 48.2 cm
(Not in the exhibition)

of a female god in the process of labour, was so controversial to British audiences that it was regularly the focus of police complaints. Similarly an etching by Cooper, *Tree of Life*, 1986, shows a floating female figure who holds a tree in her hand and a baby crawling to the left of the paper, and here the mother, though present, is a universal figure, one observing the universe for which she has ultimate responsibility but holding it tentatively and at arm's length from her elevated position to contemplate the messy, visceral, creative, infuriating process of life-giving and support.

Her works from the 1990s focus more on lone figures, presumably enabled by her children's schooling offering more space and time for her solo pursuits. *Woman Examining her Shadow*, 1989–90, and a series of drawings *Woman Rebuilding Herself*, 1991, reflect back on her work from the 1970s and explorations of identity. The woman remains at the centre of everything, she is naked and dislocated, placing a severed head onto the naked body of another version of herself or that of another woman, exploring an alien moonlit landscape, searching for her own reflection.

> *The transition from my mother to a living corpse had been definitively accomplished. The world had shrunk to the size of her room: When I crossed Paris by taxi I saw nothing more than a stage with extras walking on it. My real life took place at her side, and it had only one aim – protecting her.*[5]

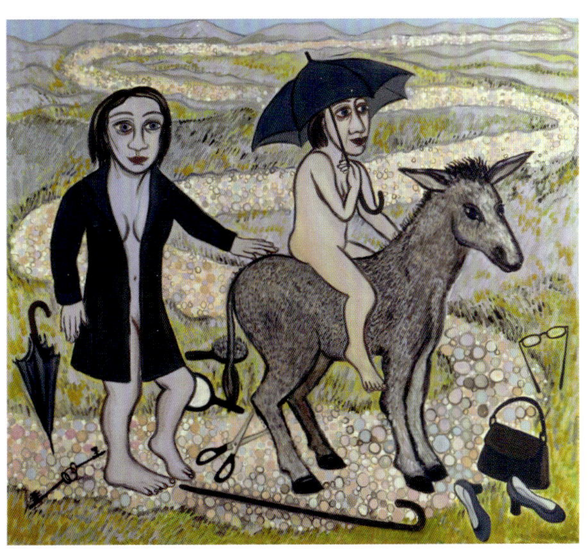

All Roads Lead... 2003 (p. 111)

A mother's death is one of the most unspoken experiences but perhaps the most profound. Whether a loving or distant relationship, the experience, particularly for a daughter, is one that upends reality. It follows that Cooper, with her devotion to sharing female experience, would give it a face within her practice.

All Roads Lead..., 2003 depicts two women, one partially clothed and the other naked and making a journey on a donkey's back. This painting and its sisters are about the death of Cooper's mother, here journeying to some other realm; glasses, hairbrush, handbag and heels cast aside and motioned on by her companion's steady hand. The donkey seems unsure but the woman astride him touches his neck, gently urging motion toward the road ahead. The limited number of paintings which depict the passing of mothers are devotional portraits of bodies but Cooper's series of pastels invoke the constellation of emotions that constitute a death, firmly in the experience of the living. The mother, daughter, animals and natural world are one and becoming closer through the shedding of worldly objects. In doing this it evokes the wild multitude of emotions the experience entails, the strange joy of supporting a loved one's end of life, the tenderness of caring for a body and the administration of objects that so often falls to a female family member, navigating the practical machinations of death while emotions rage. Like so many of Cooper's works it focussed on a period of extraordinary private destruction and regrowth, one that is horribly inevitable but is rarely regarded as a subject for work.

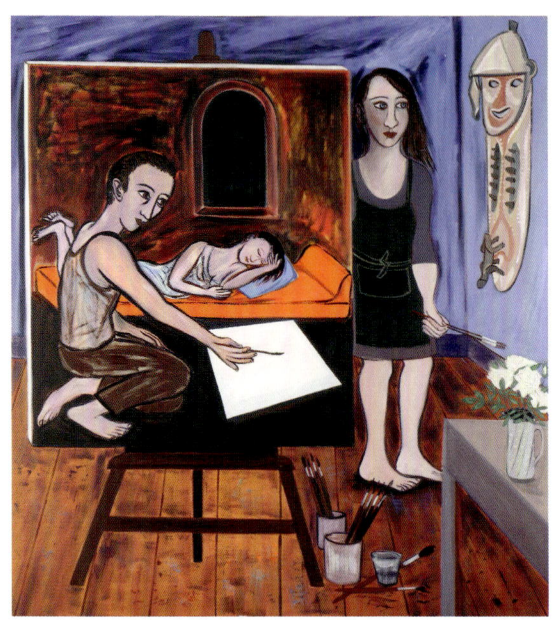

Night Studio 2010
Oil on canvas, 153 × 137 cm
(Not in the exhibition)

In 2010, after decades of teaching in art schools, Cooper would become the first female Keeper of the Royal Academy with responsibility for the highly regarded RA Schools, where she would remain until stepping down in 2017. Cooper's work from this time shows renewed vigour and an increased stylisation of forms. Works such as *The Big Painting*, 2011, *Night Studio*, 2010 and *The Red Line*, 2012, bring us into the studio, where the process of women's artistic labour is captured and shared. There is a clarity and directness to these images that perhaps reflects the experience of ageing and the matured confidence it delivers. Cooper has spoken about the decisively female energy that she brought into her professional life, a mode of working focused on listening and paying particular attention to those who seemed to be on the margins or whose work was criticised for those heinous crimes of appearing decorative or sentimental. A series of portraits of students begun in 2018 shows the closeness and trust she attained with a new generation of artists and her celebration of the increasing diversity of the visual arts in Britain.

Be it a focus on sex, birth, death or work, Cooper presents an experience of the world that is infinitely complex and layered. Across painting, drawing, collage and printmaking she has built, and continues to build, a world that truthfully reflects the daily experiences of women and celebrates their messy, painful thrill. Whilst she has often insisted that her female characters are all women and not direct representations of herself, a recent work, *Self Portrait with Toys*, 2018 (p. 65) gives us a glimpse of the woman behind the canvas. Dressed in a polka dot shirt, wearing spectacles and greying hair cut into a short bob, she scrutinises herself in a mirror, in front of which three small children's toys sit upon a shelf. The roles of mother, lover, provider and caregiver within the domestic realm is one that she will always staunchly defend.

Notes:
1. Anne Boyer, *Garments Against Women*, Ashata Press, Boise, Idaho, 1973 p. 9
2. *The Guardian*, October 1980
3. John Spurling, *New Statesman*, 17th October 1980
4. Rachel Cusk, *A Life's Work*, Faber and Faber, London, 2019 p. 58
5. Simone De Beauvoir, *A Very Easy Death*, André Deutsch Ltd., George Weidenfeld and Nicolson Ltd., and G. P. Putnam's Sons, 1965, 1985 edition p. 73

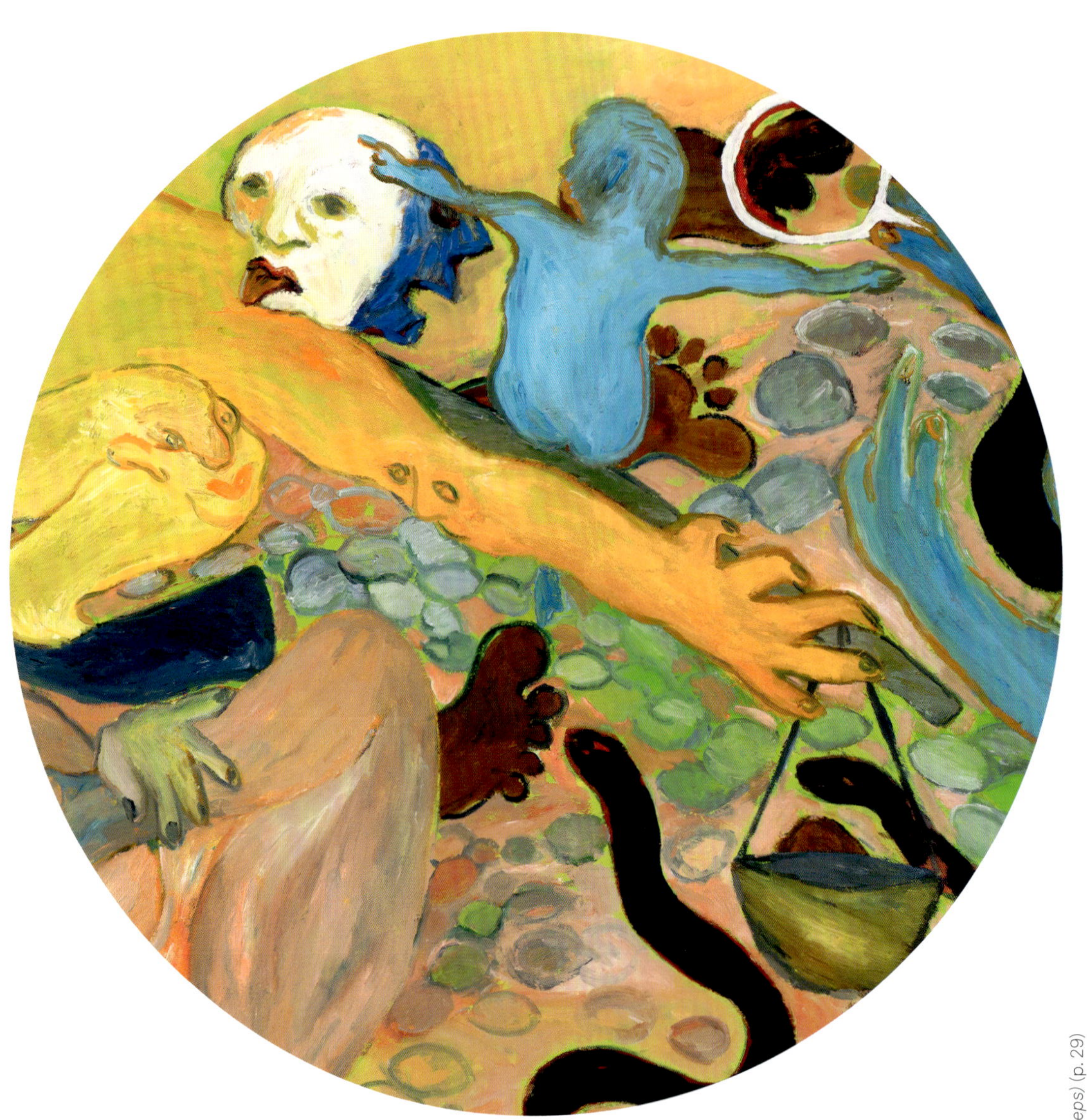

Detail: *Clued In (Following in Footsteps)* (p. 29)

1 EARLY YEARS

Art studies took Cooper to London, Goldsmiths and the RCA, where her education embraced the legacy of Abstraction, Pop and Conceptual art. She emerged into a world of Neo-Expressionism, reacting to the detached coolness of what had come before with a renewed interest in emotion and storytelling. In her time as a student Cooper had very few female role models with the art scene dominated by men. Feminist artists, like Judy Chicago, were turning their backs on painting and looking to new media, yet artists like Cooper and Paula Rego, friends and contemporaries, persisted with their preferred medium and with a mutual interest in a cast of unusual characters and animals.

While Cooper's work contains a strong autobiographical element, allegorical and poetic in its storytelling, the concerns and experiences that she depicts are timeless and universal. A strong colourist and often described as a magic realist, Cooper brings an unapologetically female perspective to her subject matter, encompassing raw sexuality, motherhood, life and death. Similarly, Peter Doig, who was taught by Cooper when he attended St Martin's, continues to be interested in the creation of rich, curious narratives.

The heightened palette of Cooper's early work owes something to her encounter with Leicester Museums' *Red Woman* by Franz Marc, which Cooper remembers seeing while teaching in the city. As she has commented, 'In the precious hours when my new baby slept, I remember being obsessed with red, reaching for it instinctively and moulding these paintings from cadmium, sienna and crimson. The female figures getting bigger and bigger.' Cooper's naked red figures are not sexualised but are intended as representations of strong, working women – nurturing children, tending plants, climbing trees. Their tilted heads with solemn, yet gentle expressions adding to the tenderness that she sees in these capable and industrious women.

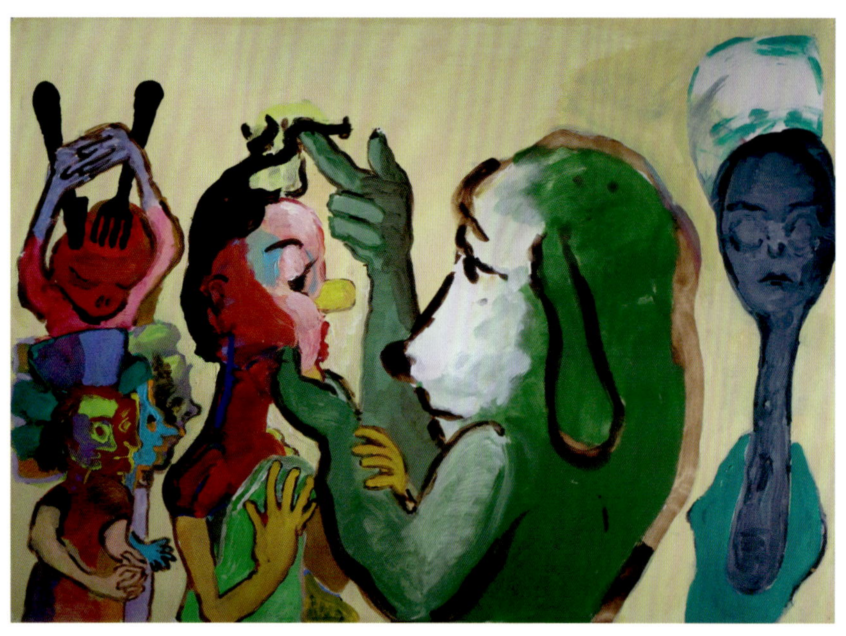

PAULA REGO
(1935–2022)

1
Three Guchi Faces, Guchi Face with Cutlery 1983
Acrylic on paper, 76.5 × 101.5 cm

Leicester Museums & Galleries: Purchased from Mrs Monika Kinley with assistance from the MGC/V&A Purchase Grant Fund, 1984

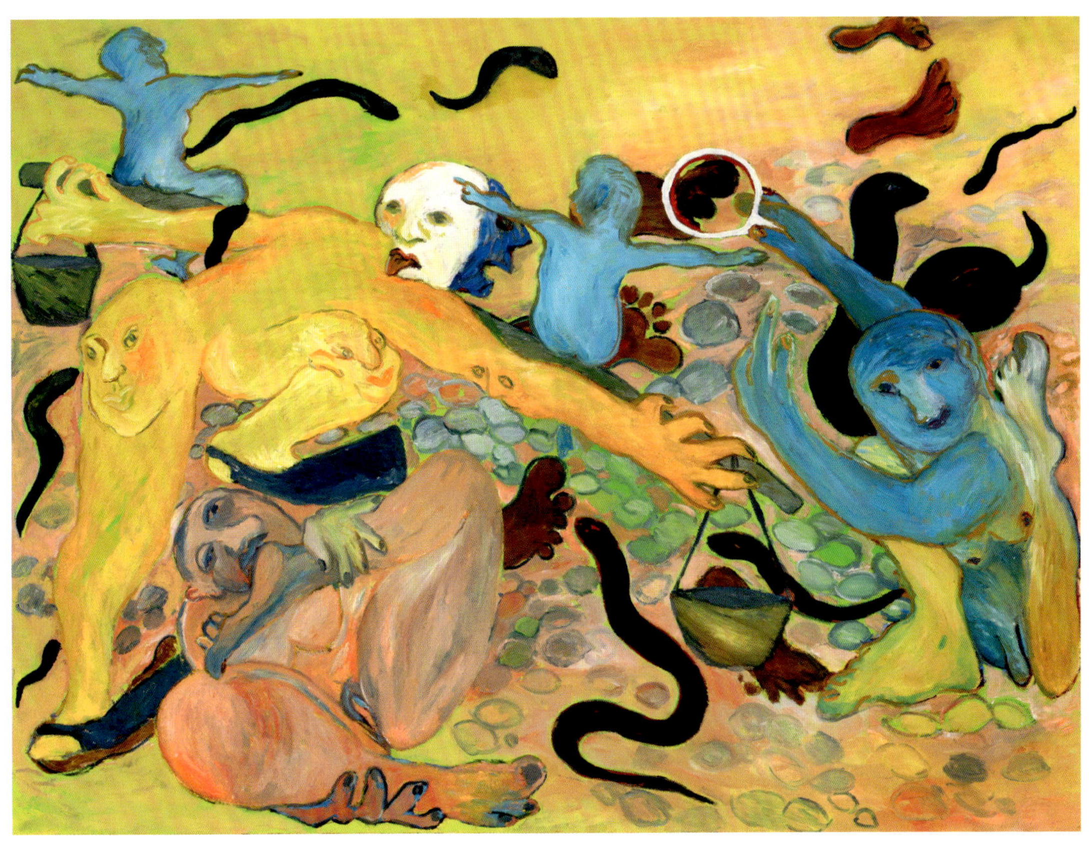

2
Clued In (Following in Footsteps) 1980
Oil on canvas, 136 × 182 cm

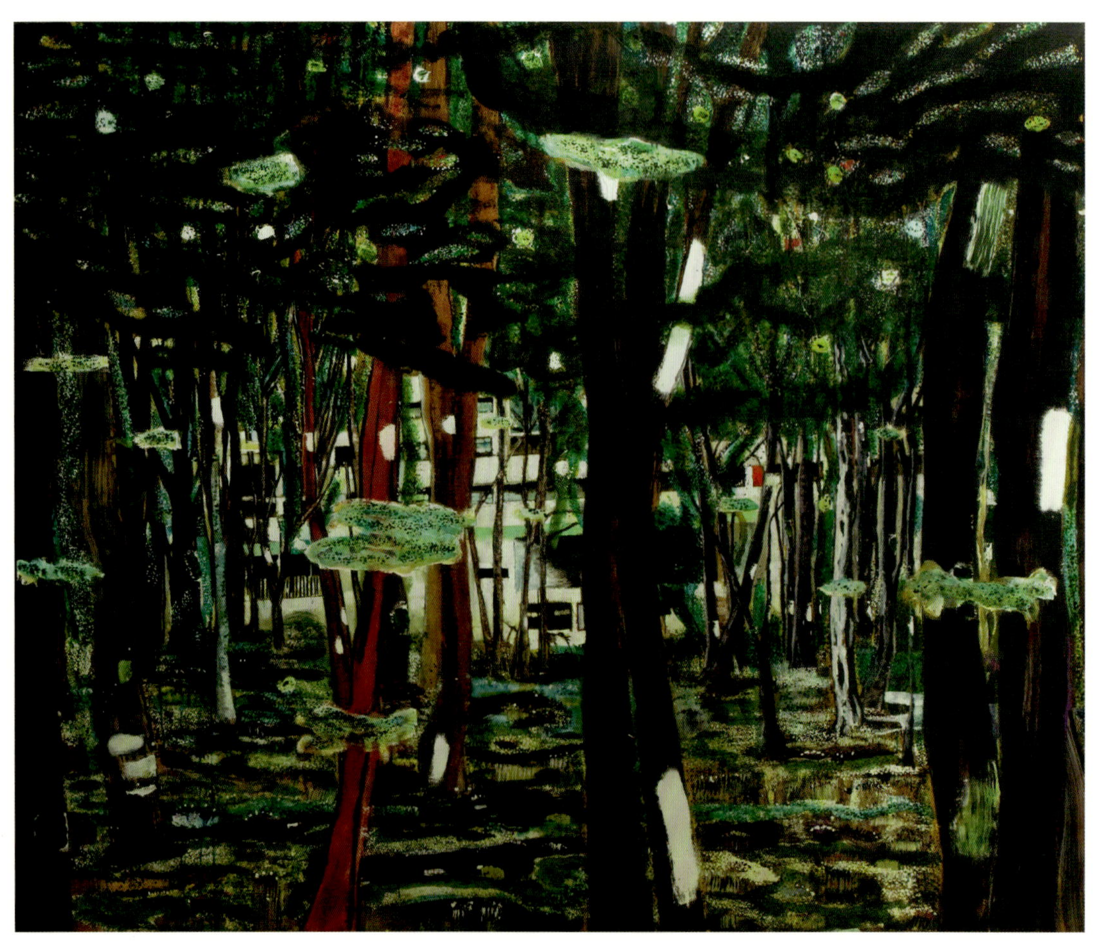

PETER DOIG
(b. 1959)

3
Concrete Cabin 1991–2
Oil on canvas, 200.5 × 241 cm

Leicester Museums & Galleries: Gift of the Contemporary Art Society, 1996

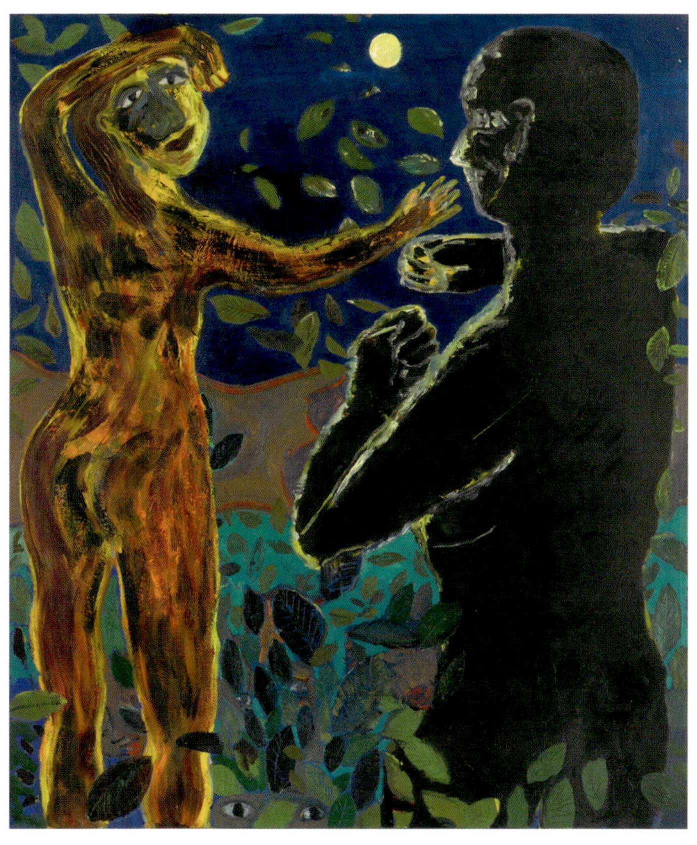

4
Going Ape 1982
Oil on canvas, 167 × 143.8 cm

Arts Council Collection, Southbank Centre, London

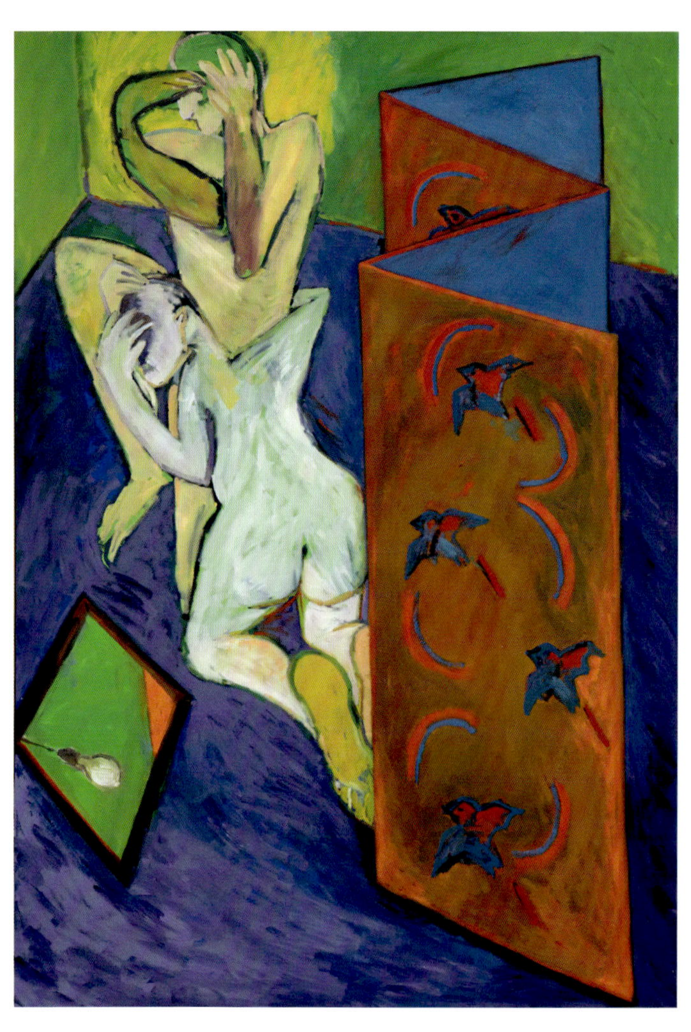

5
The Screen 1980
Oil on canvas, 157 × 111 cm

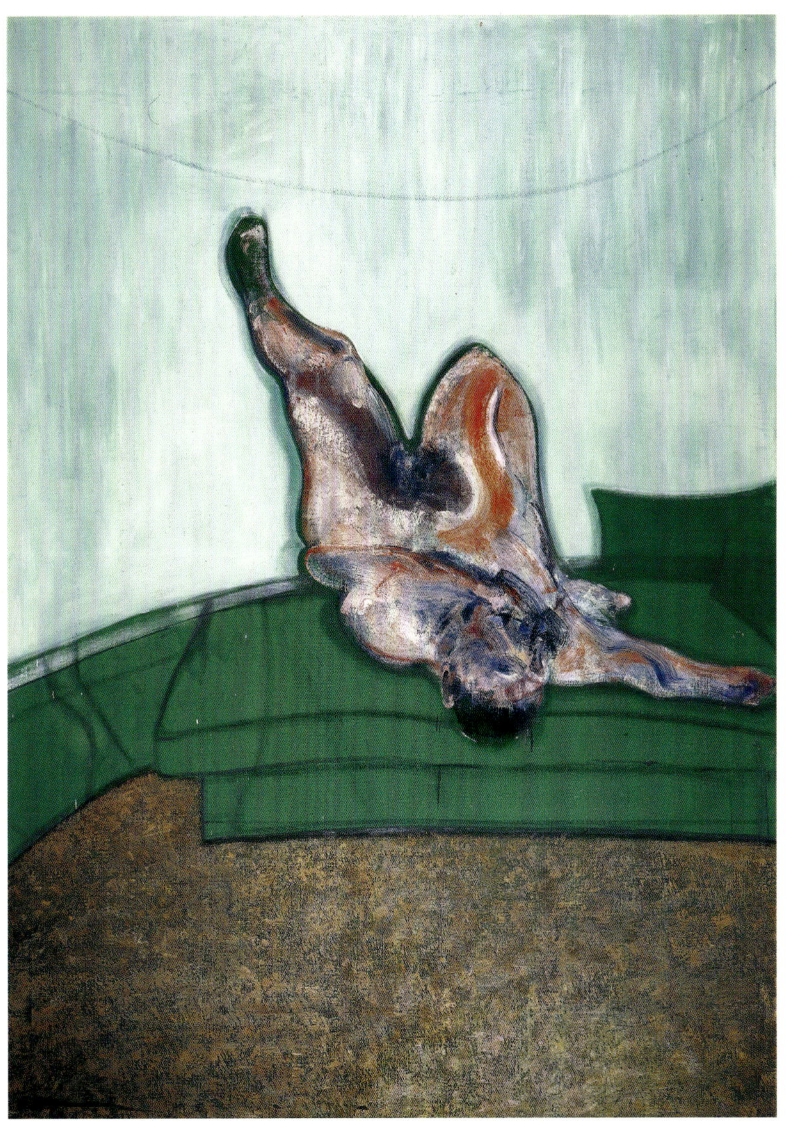

FRANCIS BACON
(1909–92)

6
Lying Figure No 1 1959
Oil on canvas, 198 x 141.5 cm

Leicester Museums & Galleries: Purchased from Marlborough Fine Art Ltd with assistance from the MGC/V&A Purchase Grant Fund, 1960

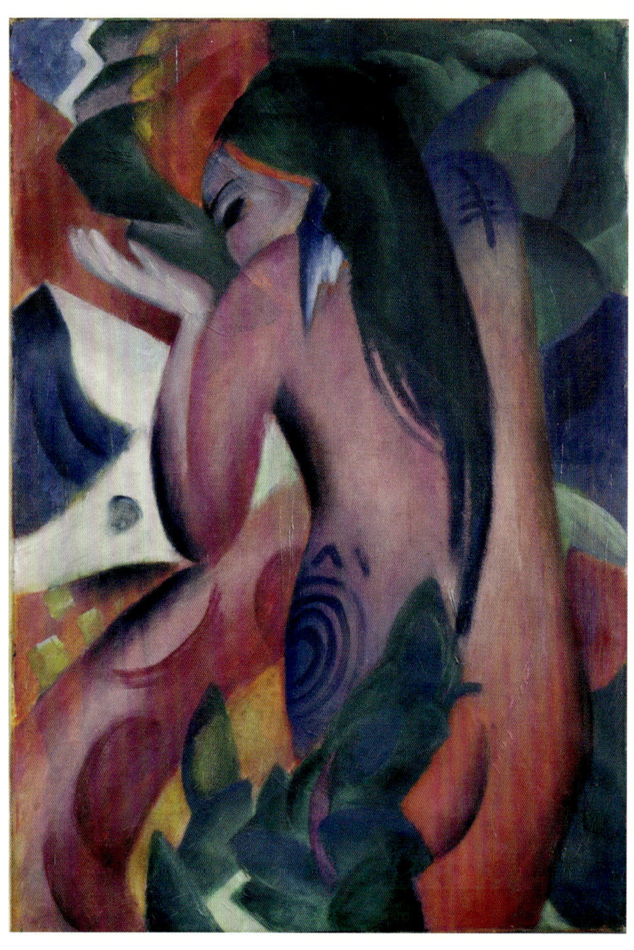

FRANZ MARC
(1880–1916)

7
Red Woman 1912
Oil on canvas, 100.5 × 70 cm

Leicester Museums & Galleries:
Purchased from Stefan Pauson, 1944

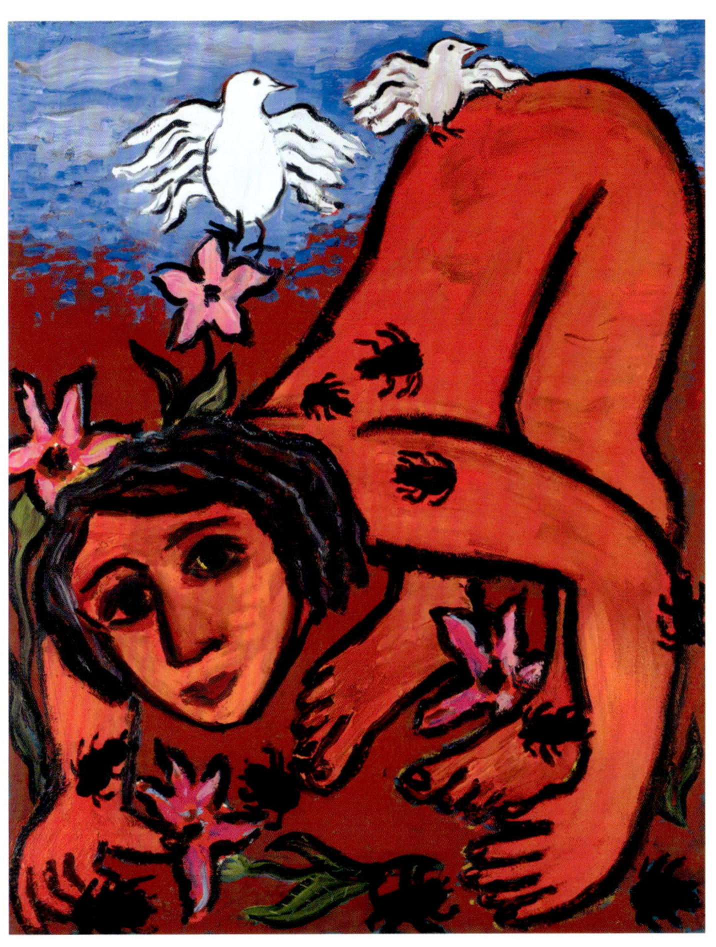

8
Creepy Crawly 1987
Oil on canvas, 91.4 × 71.1 cm

Eileen Cooper Family Collection

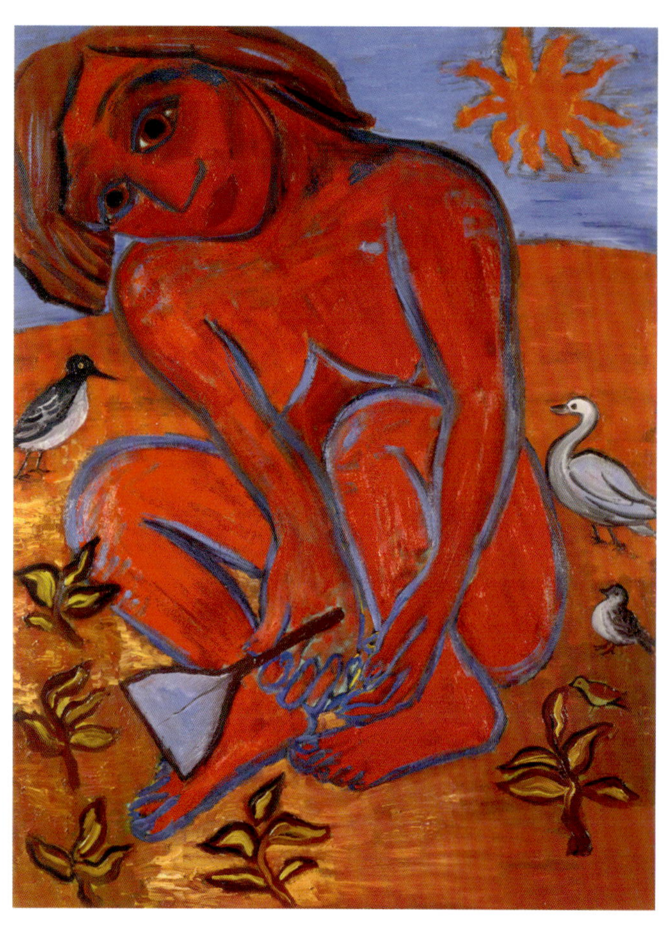

9
Pick of the Crop 1987
Oil on canvas, 122 × 91.5 cm

Private Collection

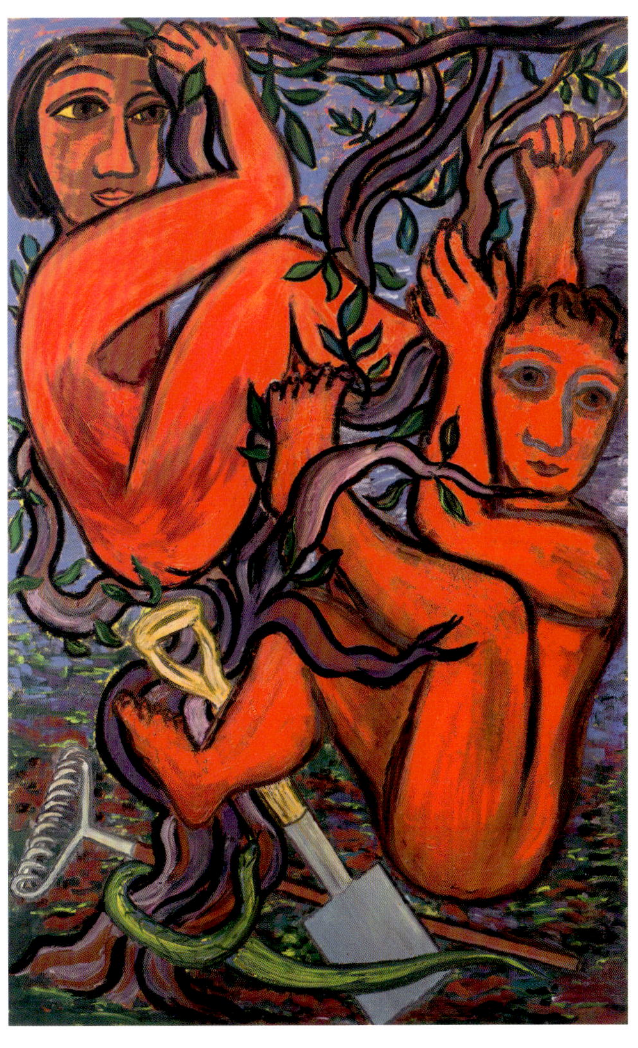

10
The Two Gardeners 1989
Oil on canvas, 167.5 × 106.5 cm

Private Collection

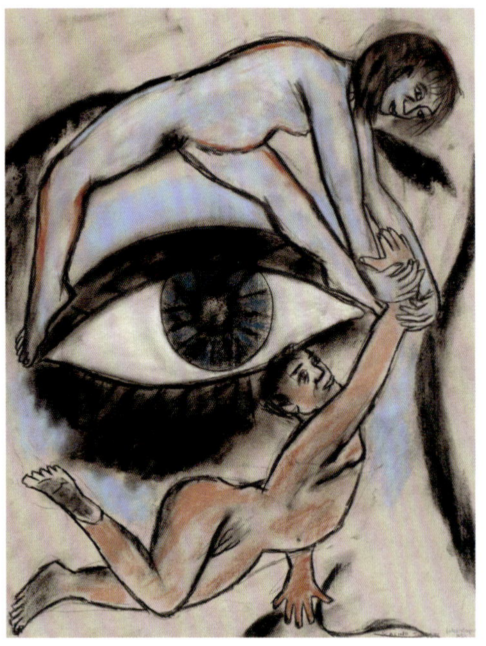

i

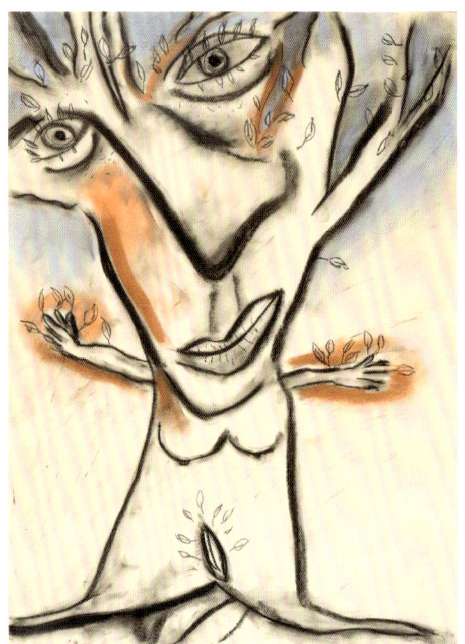

ii

i *Scaling the Eye*, 1981, Conté, charcoal and pastel on paper, 65 × 50 cm
ii *The Sad Tree*, 1983, Conté, charcoal and pastel on paper, 63.5 × 47 cm
iii *Footprints*, 1988, oil on canvas, 86 × 152.5 cm
iv *Woman in Tree*, 1989, monoprint, 110 × 78 cm
v *Treasury*, 1985, oil on canvas, 244 × 183 cm

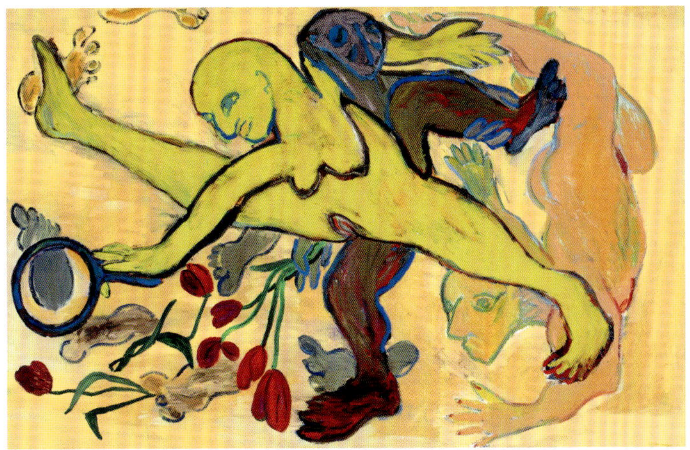

iii

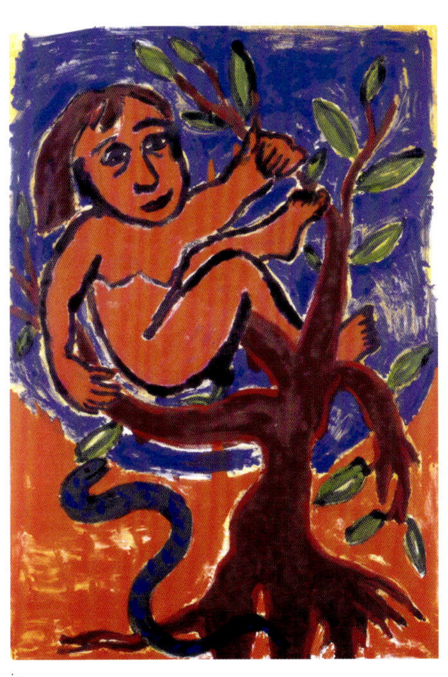

iv

v

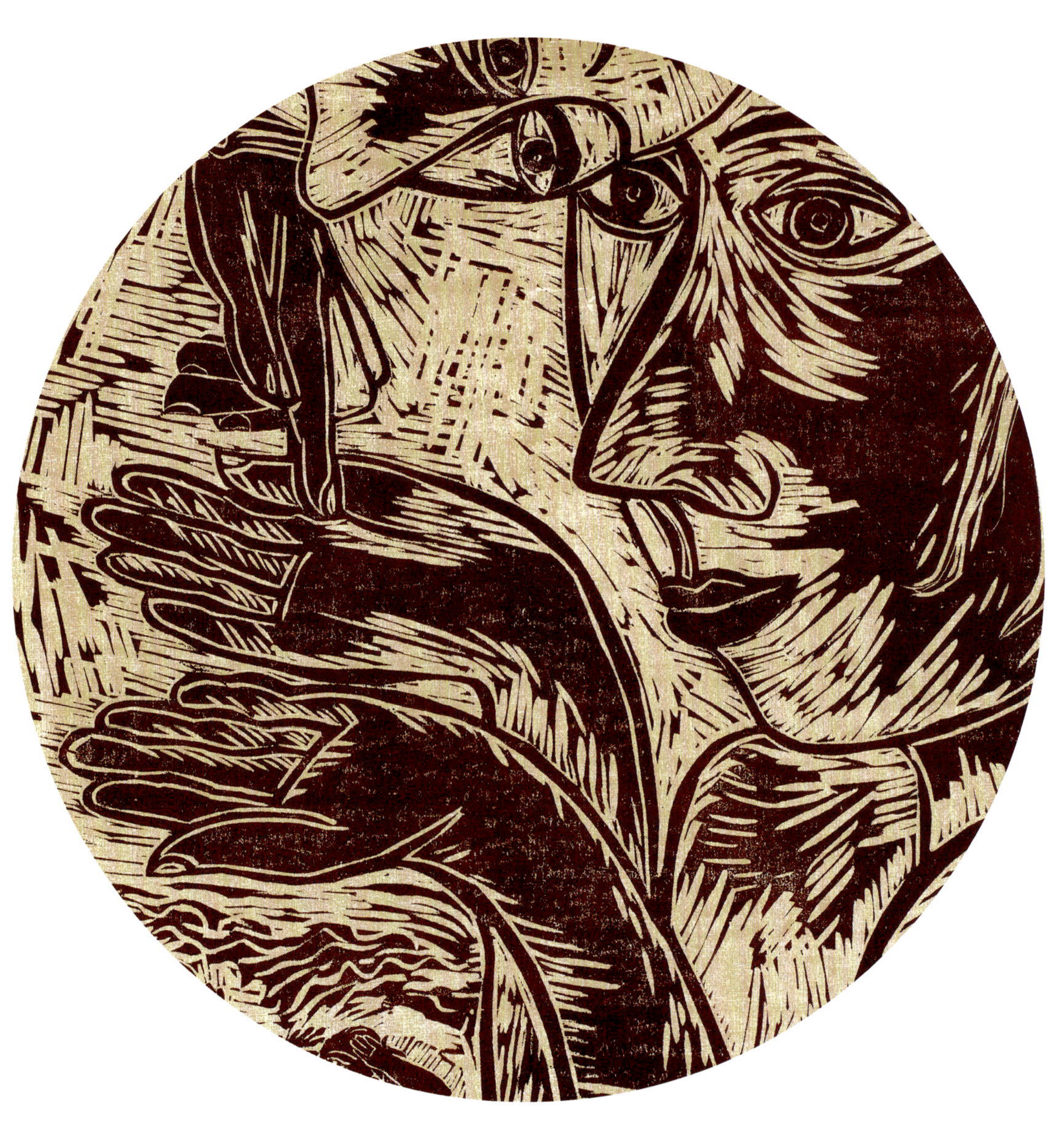

Detail: *Spellbound* (p. 45)

2 PRINTMAKING AND GERMAN EXPRESSIONISM

It was while studying at the RCA that Cooper discovered German Expressionism, seduced by its colour, movement and sexuality, specifically seeking out its celebrated female artists like Paula Modersohn-Becker and Käthe Kollwitz.

Parallels between German Expressionist printmaking and Cooper's work can be seen in the physical contortion and angularity of form, the mark-making, and composition within the block or plate, all contributing to the energy and often uncomfortable tension in the works.

Leicester Museums holds the largest and most significant collection of German Expressionist art in the UK. Beginning at the turn of the twentieth century in Germany, the movement is associated with two artistic groups – Die Brücke (the bridge), founded in 1905 in Dresden and headed up by Ernst Ludwig Kirchner, and Der Blaue Reiter (the blue rider), founded in Munich some five years later by Wassily Kandinsky and Franz Marc. Amid the ensuing horrors of the First World War artists would attempt to describe a new world order and would become fascinated with the sordid realities of modern urban life, the naked body and sex. At this time art underwent a dramatic transformation exploring inner emotions and tensions through symbolic colour and expressive line, very much influenced by the writings of psychoanalyst Sigmund Freud and the philosophy of Friedrich Nietzsche.

For Cooper, a prolific printmaker, the collaborative process of the medium is one of its attractions, as is her love of the materiality of the woodcut, echoing that of the German Expressionists who favoured the medium. For over 35 years she has worked with Sara Lee, and together in 2003 they started Blackbird Editions. More recently Cooper has been assisted by Julia Peintner in the final stages of proofing and in the editioning of her prints. Having lectured on printmaking at the RCA (1994–2006) and subsequently taken up the post of Head of Printmaking at the RA Schools in 2005 (until 2010), it is no surprise that the medium sits at the heart of her artistic creativity, its focus on a limited palette marking a difference with the heightened palette of her paintings.

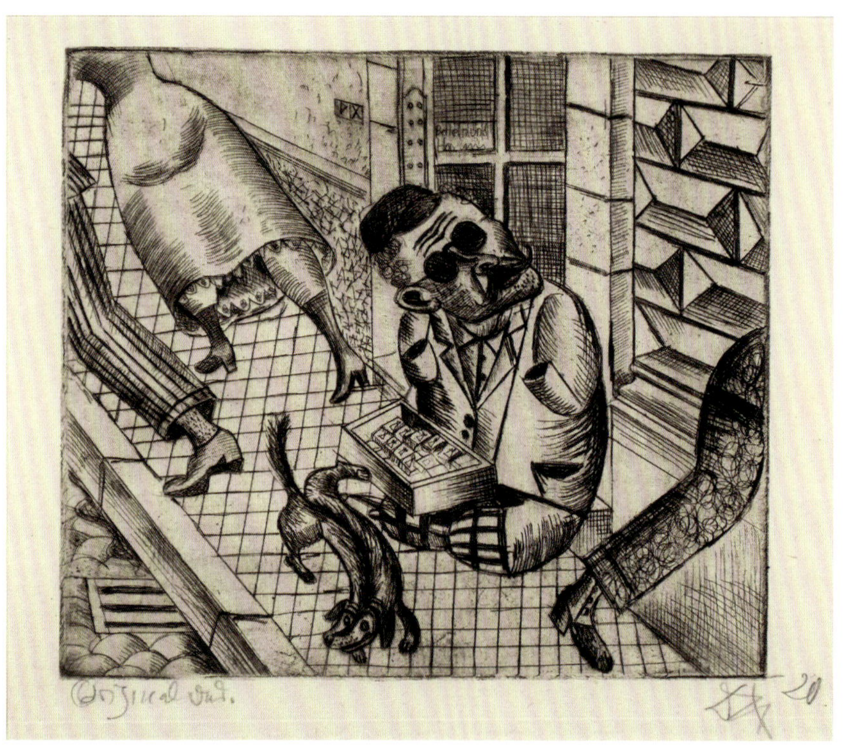

OTTO DIX
(1891–1969)

11
The Match Seller 1920
Drypoint etching, 25.6 × 29.7 cm (34.5 × 52.5 cm)

Leicester Museums & Galleries: Purchased from Christie's with assistance from the City of Leicester Museums Trust, ACE/V&A Purchase Grant Fund and The Art Fund, 2014

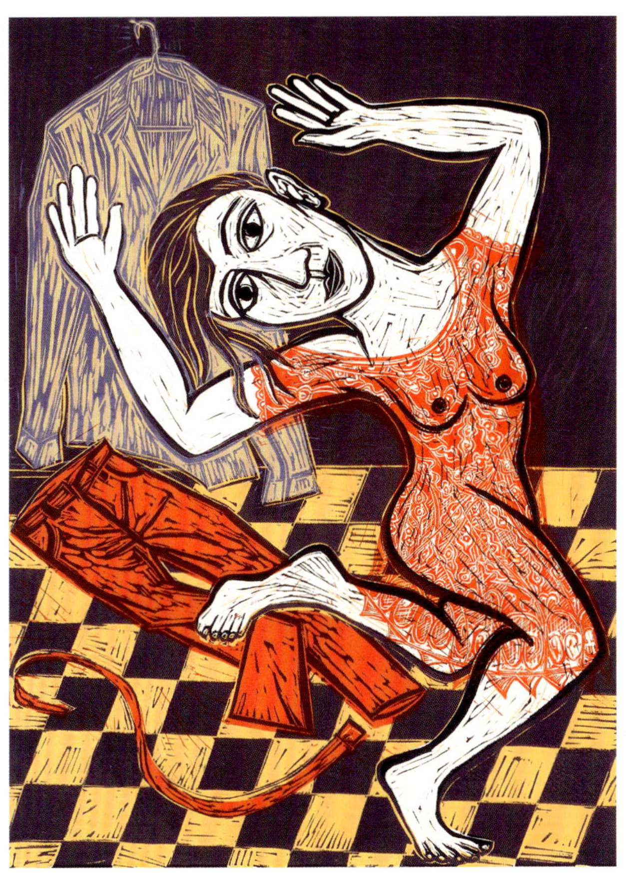

12
Red Dress 2009
Linocut, 61 × 45 cm (81 × 63 cm)

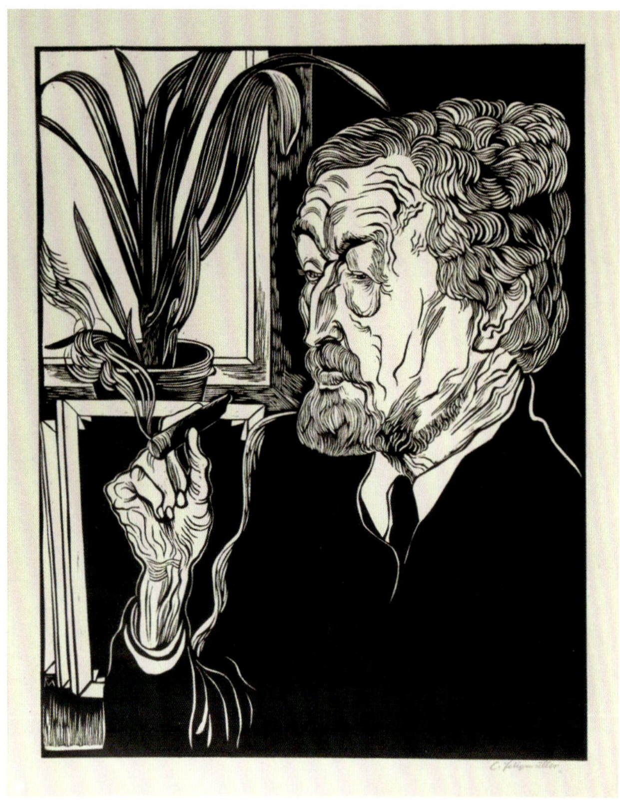

CONRAD FELIXMÜLLER
(1897–1977)

13
Portrait of Christian Rohlfs 1927
Woodcut, 49.4 × 39.7 cm (60.4 × 48.7 cm)

Leicester Museums & Galleries:
Gift of Titus Felixmüller, 1996

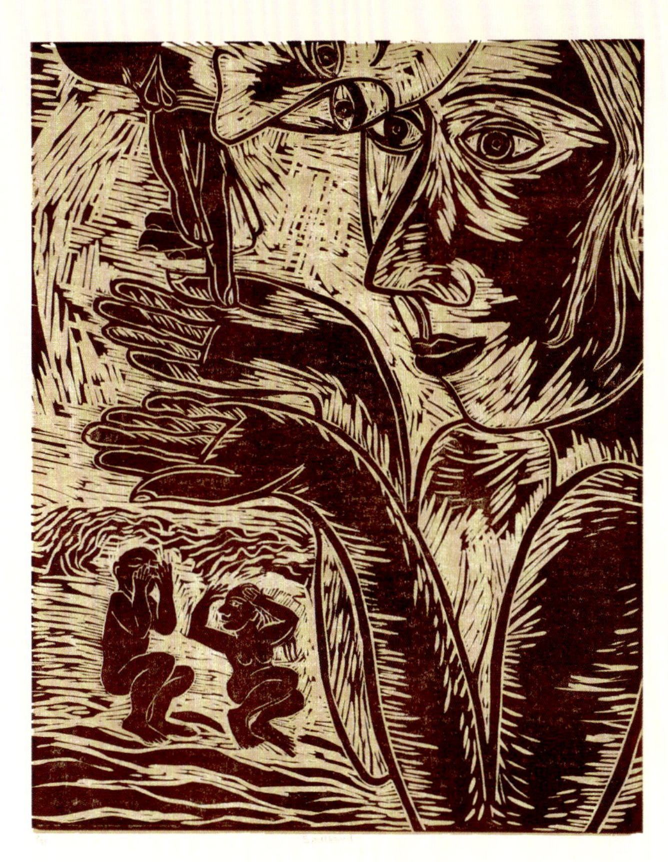

14
Spellbound 1998
Woodcut, 76 × 61 cm (95 × 76.5 cm)

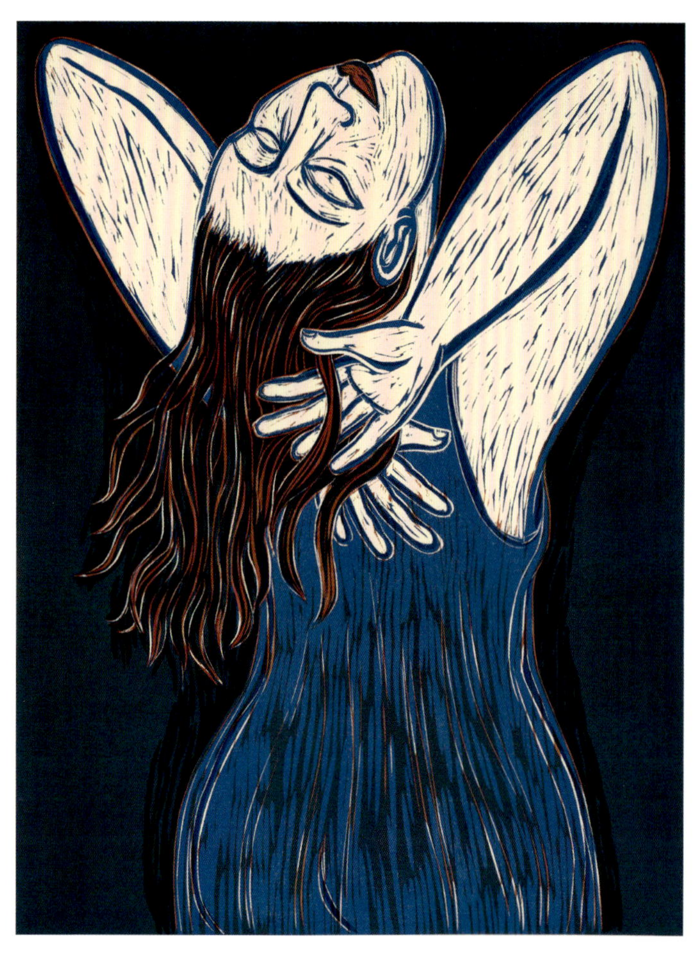

15
Celestina 2018
Woodcut, 65 × 50 cm (96 × 66.5 cm)

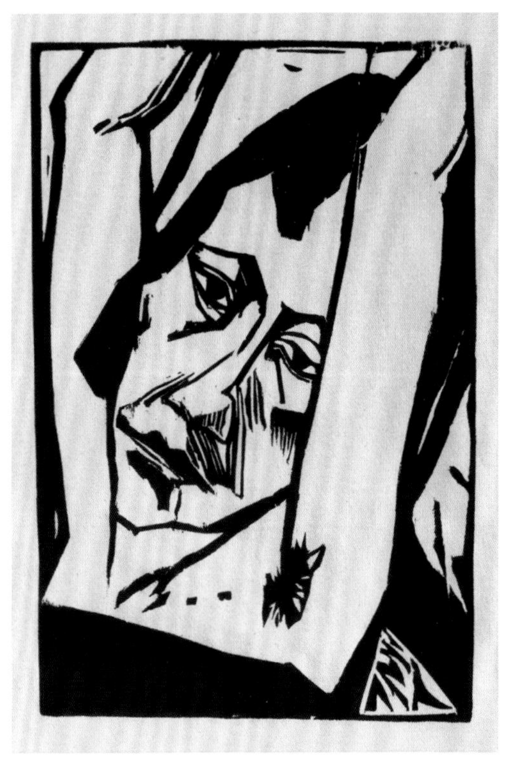

ERICH HECKEL
(1883–1970)

16
Woman with Raised Arms 1913
Woodcut, 25.8 × 17.2 cm (34.3 × 24.6 cm)

Leicester Museums & Galleries: Purchased from Humphrey Wine with assistance from the MGC/V&A Purchase Grant Fund, 1981

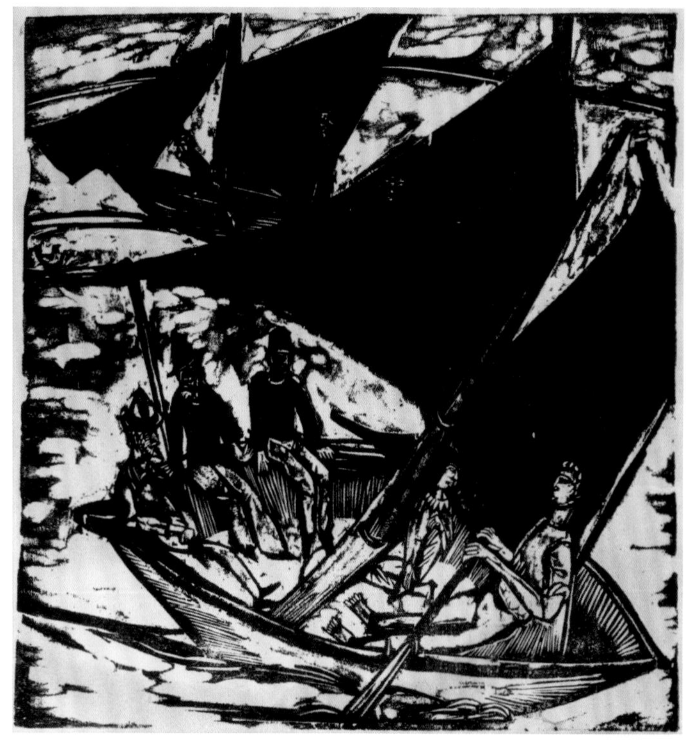

ERNST LUDWIG KIRCHNER
(1880–1938)

17
Sailing Boats off Fehmarn 1914
Woodcut, 41.8 × 39.5 cm (51.6 × 42.1 cm)

Leicester Museums & Galleries: Purchased from Robin Garton with assistance from the Art Fund, MLA/V&A Purchase Grant Fund and the City of Leicester Museums Trust, 2006

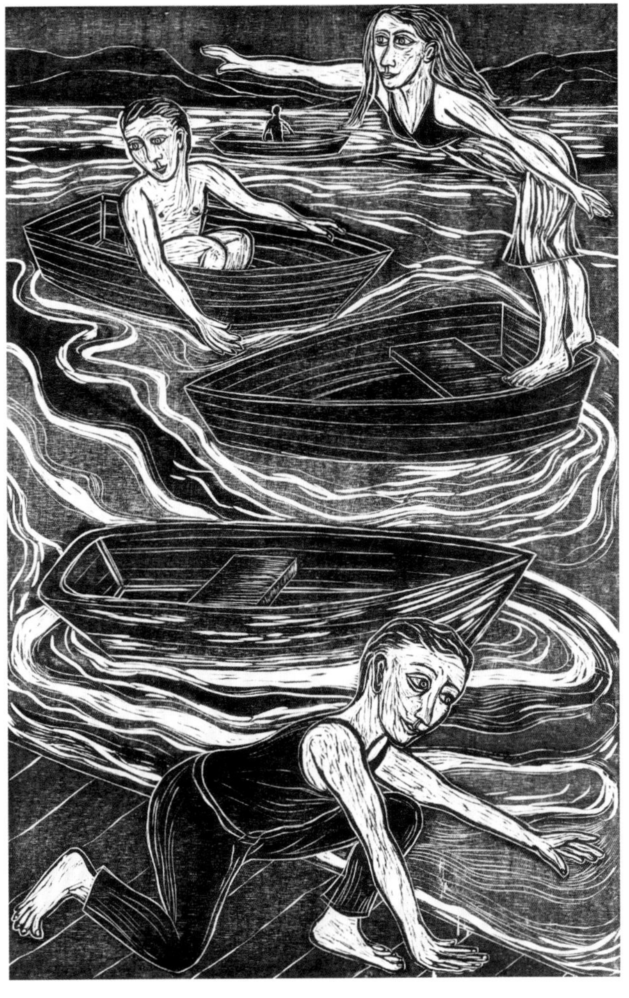

18
Cross-current 2009
Woodcut on Japanese paper, 101.5 × 60 cm (113 × 67 cm)

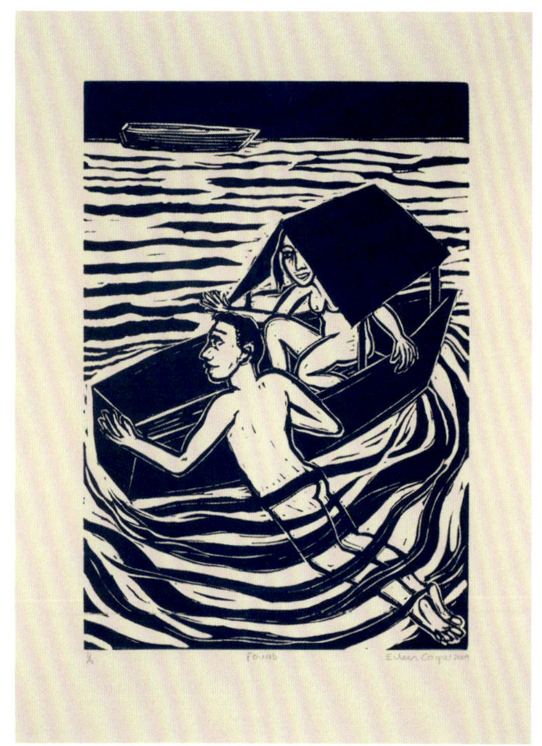

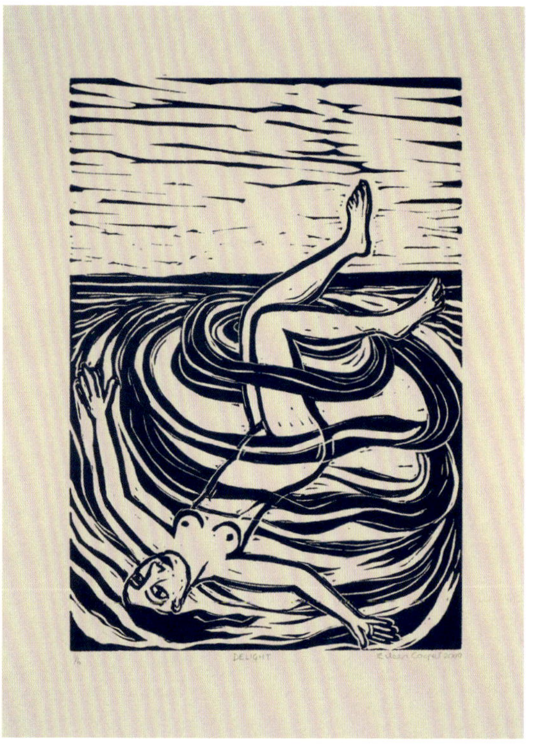

19
Delight 2009
Linocut, 30 × 21 cm (39 × 28.5 cm)

20
Found 2009
Linocut, 30 × 21 cm (39 × 28.5 cm)

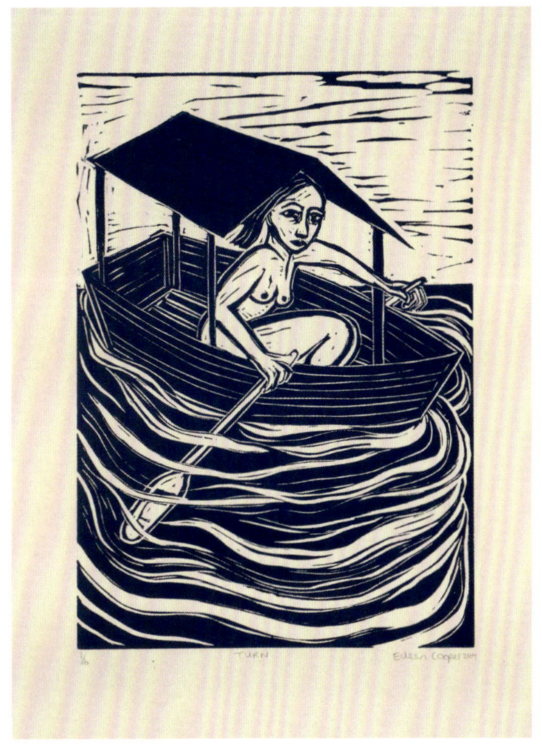

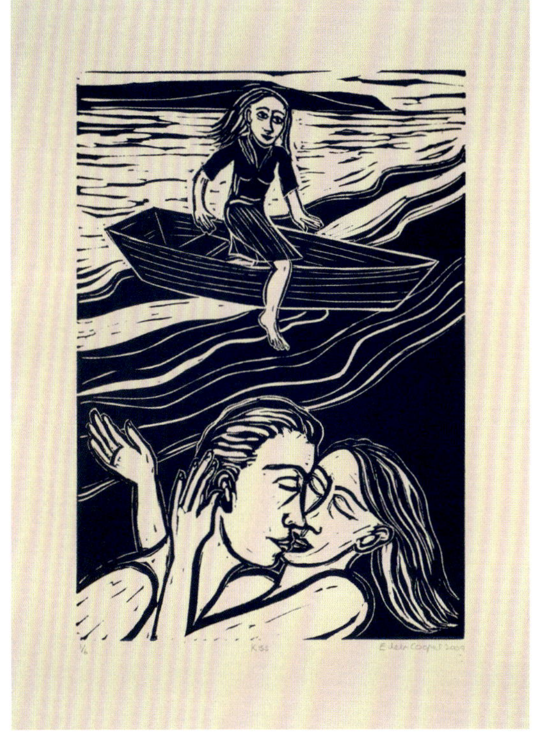

21
Turn 2009
Linocut, 30 × 21 cm (39 × 28.5 cm)

22
Kiss 2009
Linocut, 30 × 21 cm (39 × 28.5 cm)

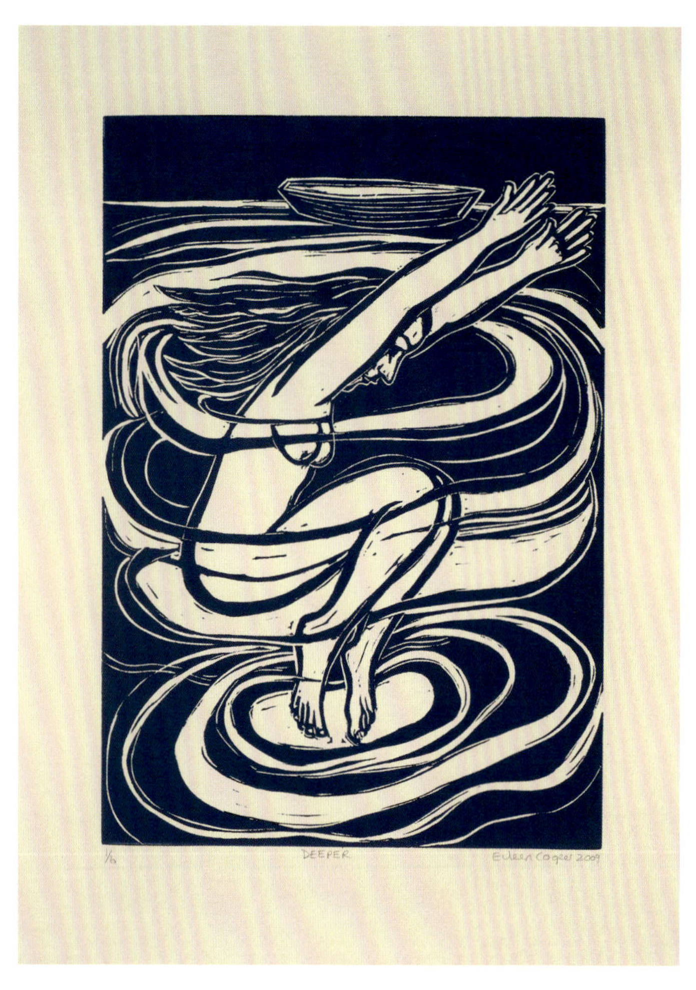

23
Deeper 2009
Linocut, 30 × 21 cm (39 × 28.5 cm)

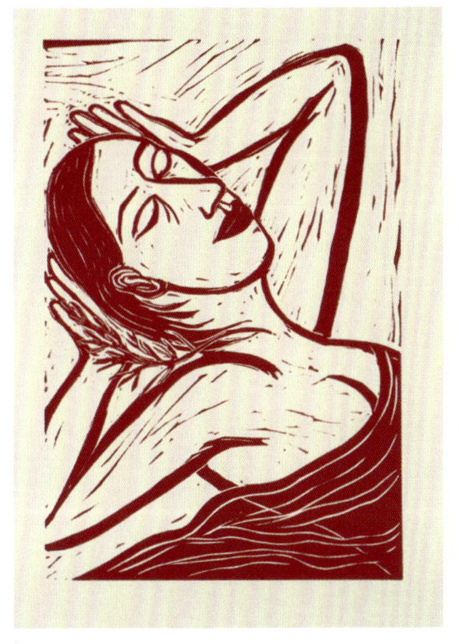

i

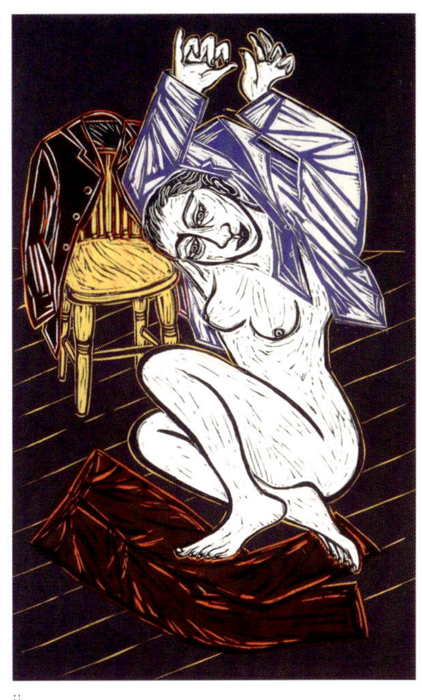

ii

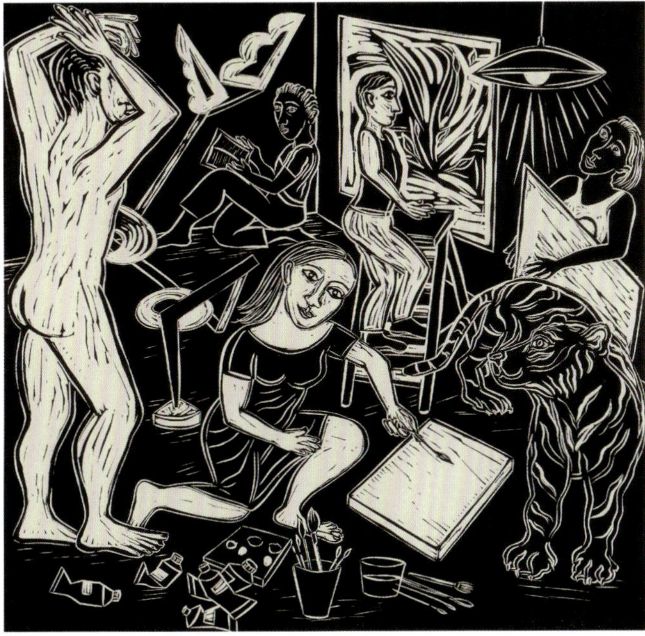

iii

i *Wildwood: Rosemary*, 2014, linocut, 33 × 23 cm (43.5 × 32 cm)
ii *With Good Grace*, 2009, linocut, 61 x 38 cm (81 × 56.5 cm)
iii *Male Model*, 2008, linocut, 51 × 51 cm

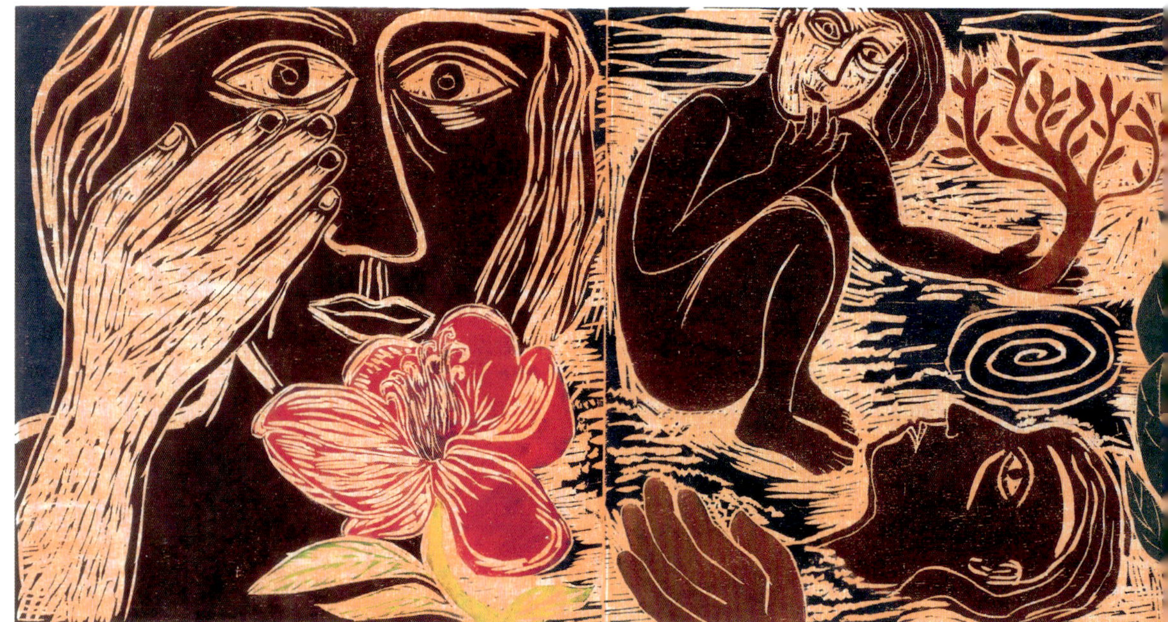

iv

iv *The Memory of a Moment*, 1996, woodcut on Japanese paper, 46 × 136 cm (66 × 156 cm)

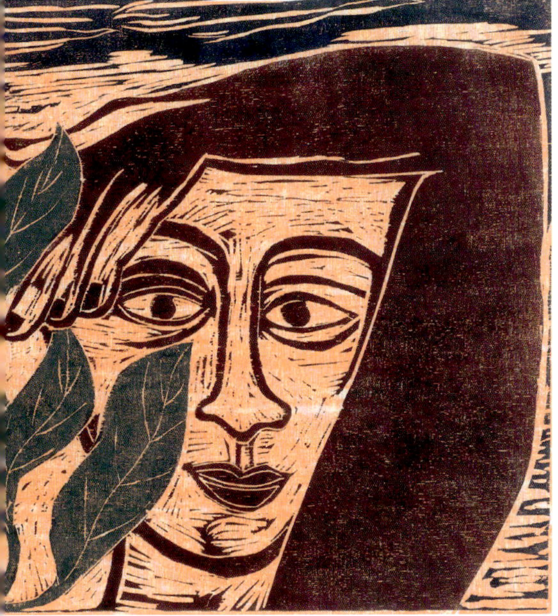

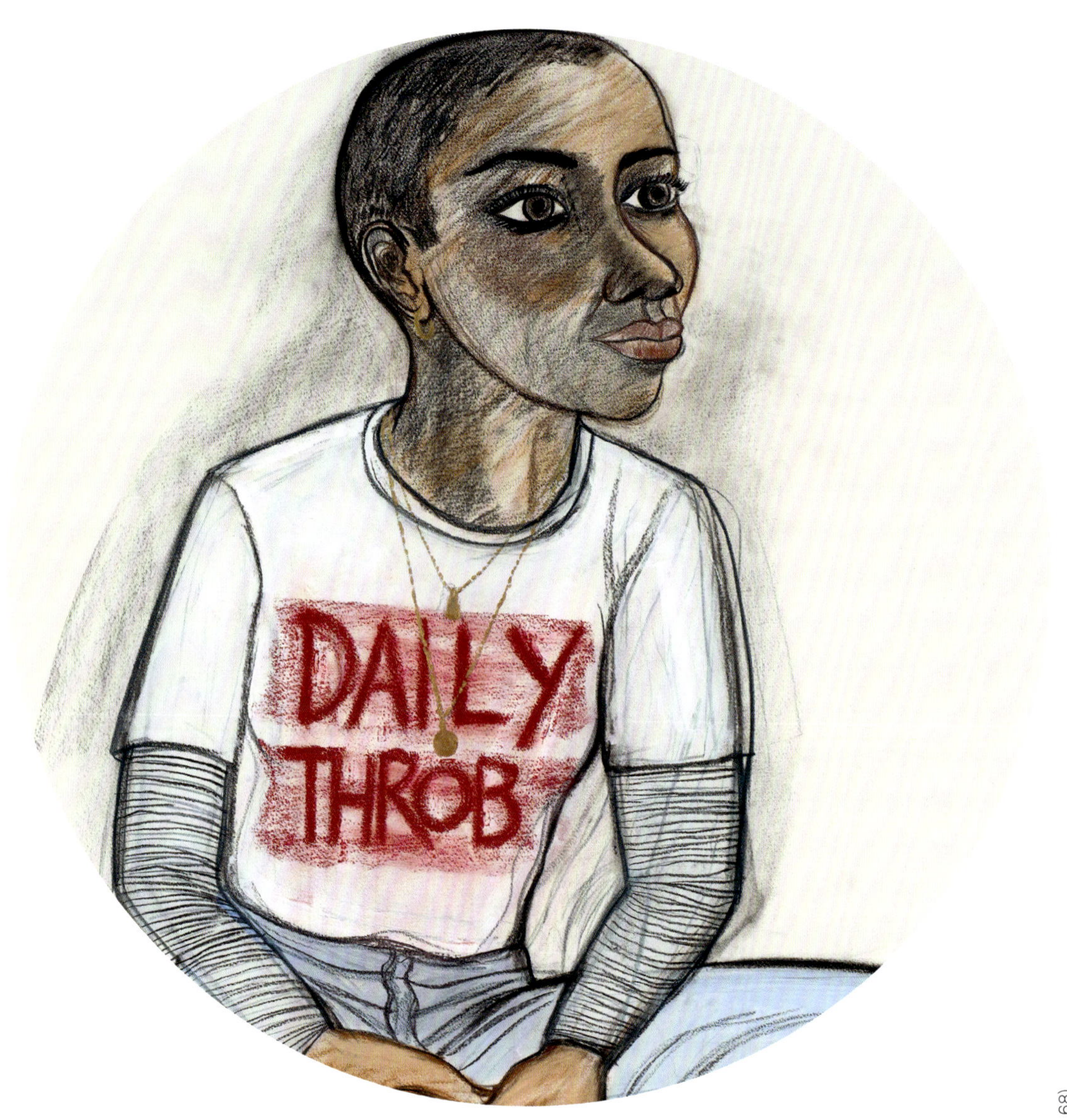

Detail: *Portrait of Rachel Jones* (p. 68)

3 LIFE

Like many women artists of her generation, seeking to find a way to make a living from their art while raising a family, Cooper taught at a number of art schools including Leicester Polytechnic, Falmouth, Camberwell, St Martin's, the RCA, City & Guilds, and the RA in London.

In balancing life and art it is no surprise that a conflation of family and imagination would occur. As with all artists, regardless of gender, the studio space plays a central role, regularly featuring in Cooper's painting and drawings. For her it is a performative space in which seemingly familiar characters feature but where the surreal presence of props or animals (especially the tiger, Cooper's alter-ego and representation of strong female creativity) abound to the point where it is easy to create a million different interpretations of each scene. The artist is more traditionally shown at work, surrounded by the tools of her trade, but less usual in that the characters are more often unclothed.

Cooper turned to self-portrait drawing in 2018, creating a suite of works reflecting her concerns as an artist approaching 70 – an exercise in intense looking and psychological investigation.

She was elected a Royal Academician in 2001 and served as Keeper of the RA between 2010 and 2017, one of four senior officers selected from the 80 Royal Academicians to oversee the institution. As such, Cooper was the first woman to be elected to the role of Keeper since the RA began in 1768. Her primary responsibility was for the RA Schools and in her time as Keeper, Cooper oversaw the transformation of its reputation so that today it is one of the most highly regarded post-graduate art schools.

In 2018, Cooper initiated a body of work capturing her young artist students from the RA Schools, many of whom are now successful in their own right. This ongoing series of drawings currently totals over 50 works and speaks clearly to Cooper's commitment to teaching and her ongoing care and support for young artists.

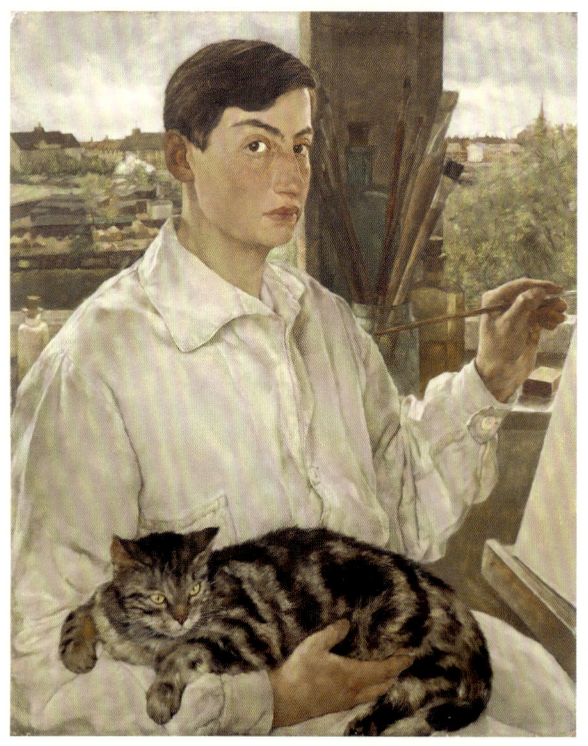

LOTTE LASERSTEIN
(1898–1993)

24
Self-portrait with a Cat, 1928
Oil on panel, 61 × 51 cm

Leicester Museums & Galleries: Purchased from the artist through Thos. Agnew and Sons Ltd, 1988

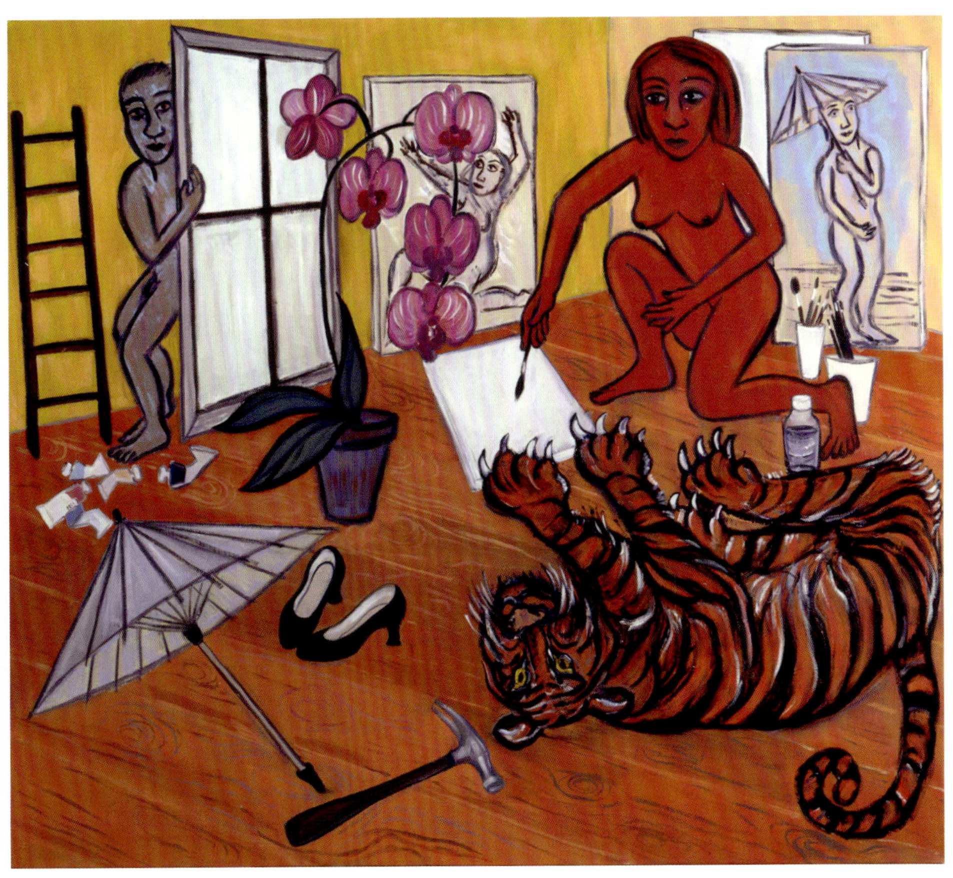

25
Studio with Tiger 2002–03
Oil on canvas, 123 × 137 cm

Private Collection

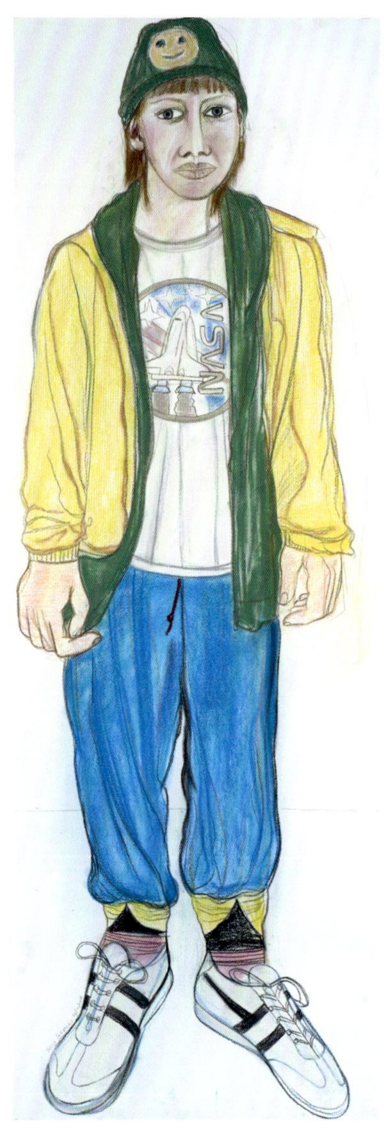

26
Jessy Jetpacks 2018
Charcoal and pastel on paper, 154 × 53 cm

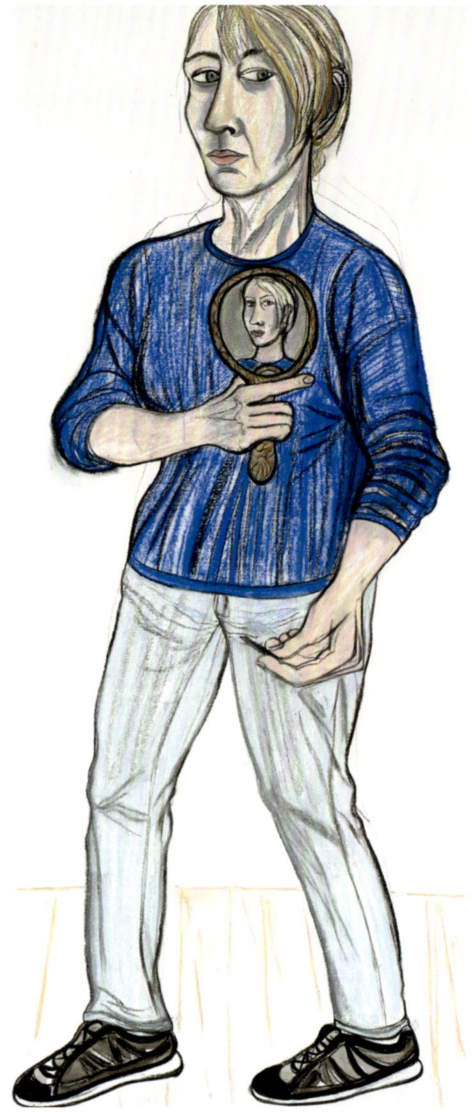

27
Portrait with Hand-mirror and Blue Jumper 2019
Charcoal and pastel on paper, 152 × 66 cm

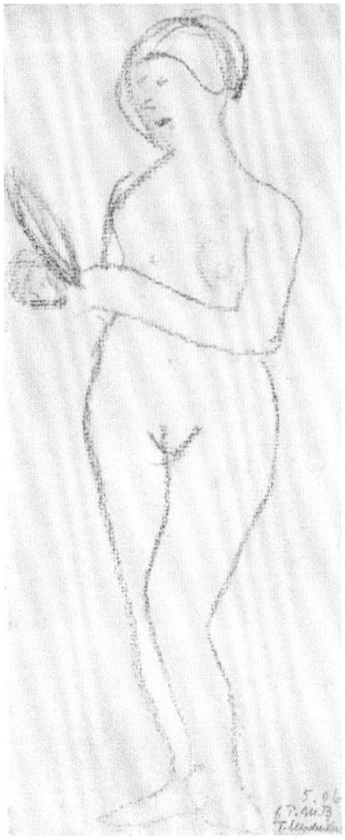

PAULA MODERSOHN-BECKER
(1876–1907)

28
Nude with a Mirror (self-portrait) 1906
Pencil on paper, 26.7 × 11.4 cm

Leicester Museums & Galleries: Purchased from the Gillian Jason Gallery, 1988

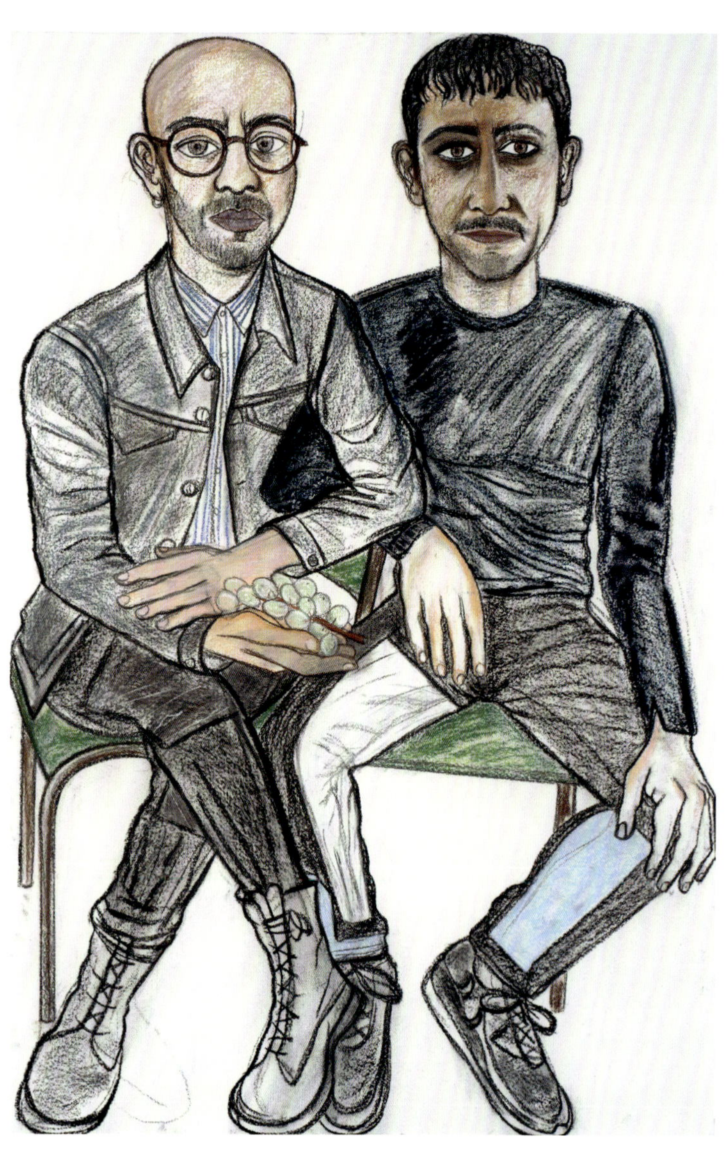

29
Joe Frazer and Prem Sahib 2019
Charcoal and pastel on paper, 152 × 101 cm

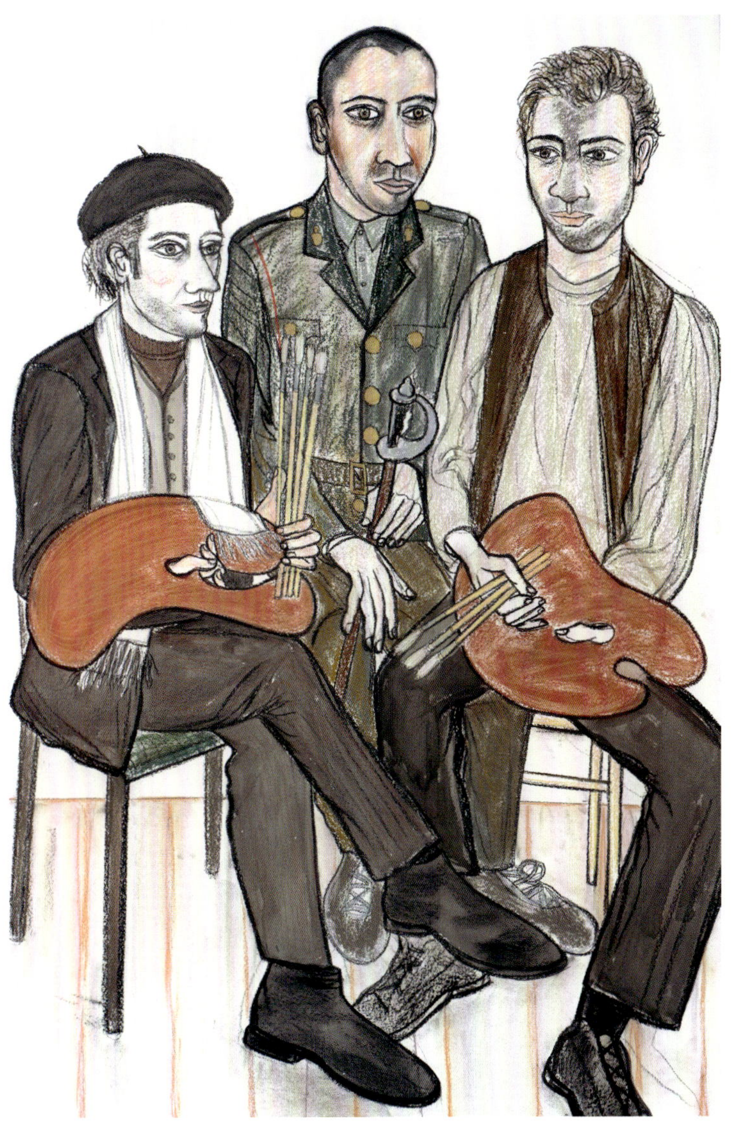

30
Max Prus, Ziggy Grudzinskas and Joel Wyllie 2019
Charcoal, pastel and watercolour on paper, 152 × 101 cm

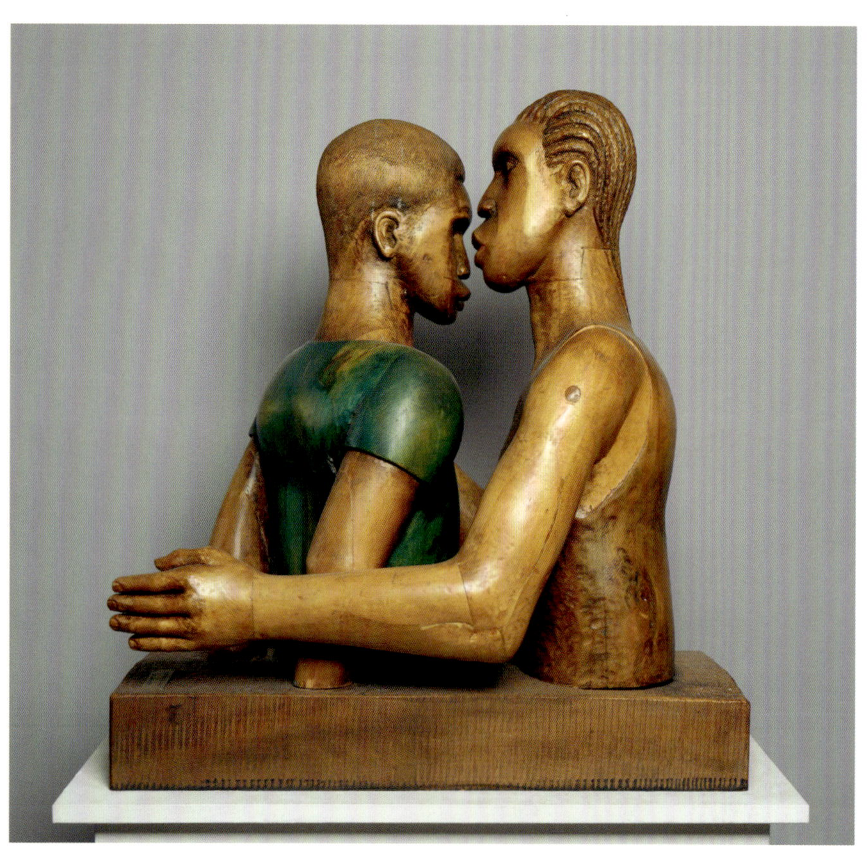

BILL MING
(b. 1944)

31
A Lesson in Trust 1985
Wood, 74.1 × 74.2 × 47 cm

Leicester Museums & Galleries: Transferred from Moat Community College, Leicester, 2006

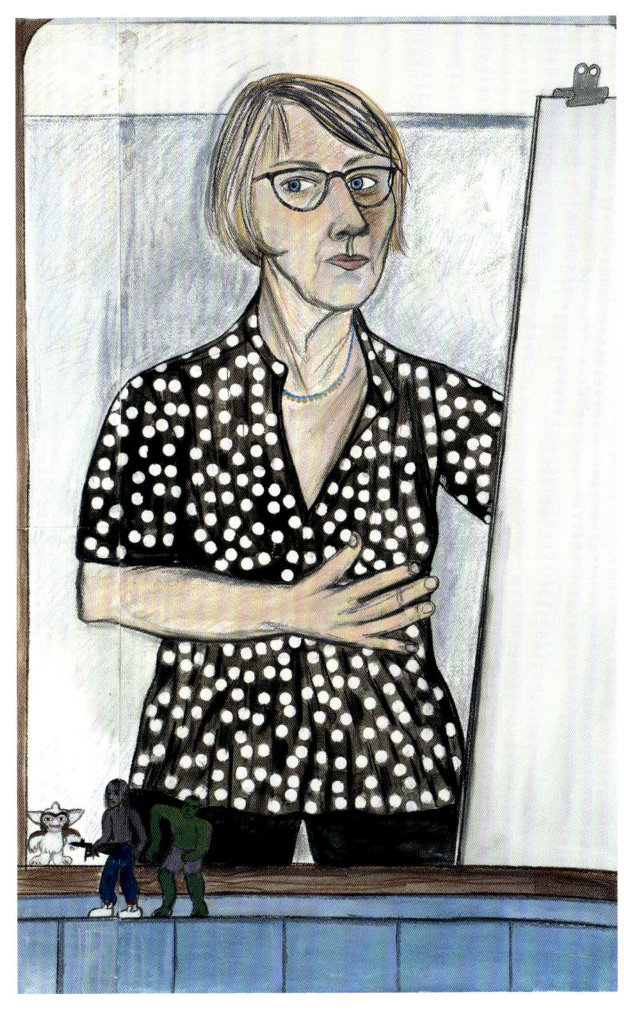

32
Self-portrait with Toys 2018
Charcoal, pastel and watercolour on paper
101.5 × 66 cm

Ruth Borchard Collection, London

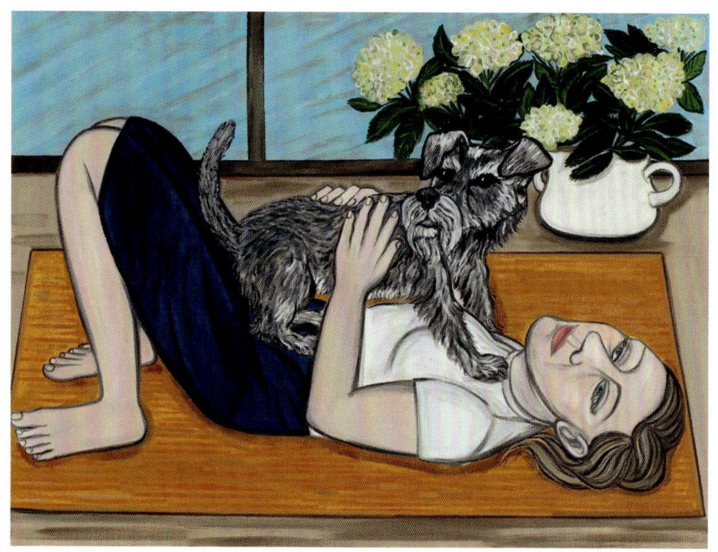

i

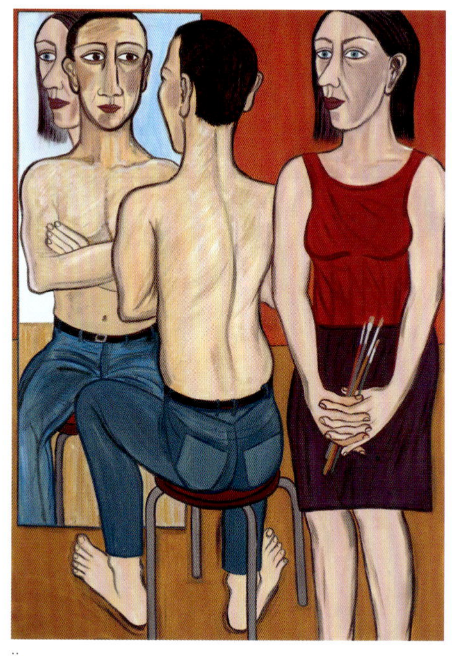

ii

i *Pause for Thought (Self-portrait with Oscar)*, 2020, oil on canvas, 90 × 120 cm
ii *Every Mother's Son*, 2019, oil on canvas, 154 × 107 cm
iii *The Black Dress*, 2019, oil on canvas, 153 × 76 cm
iv *Self-portrait with Coloured Pastels*, 2019, pastel and charcoal on paper, 60.5 × 33.5 cm

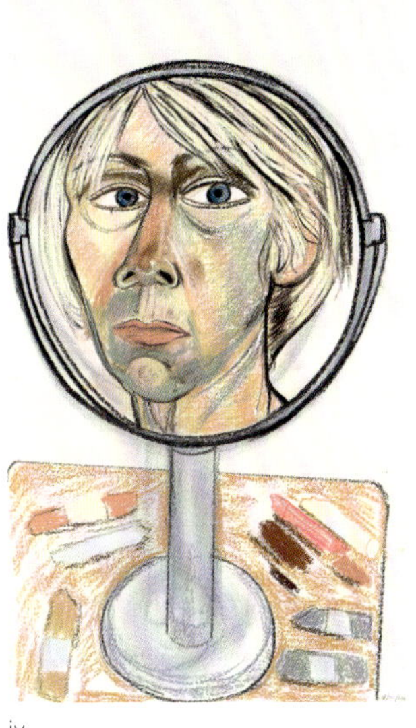
iv

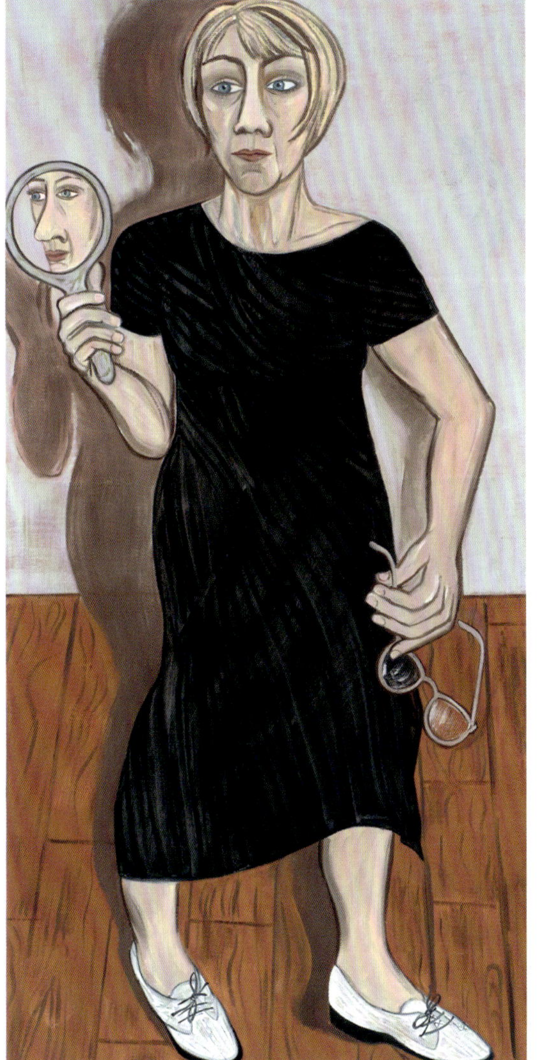
iii

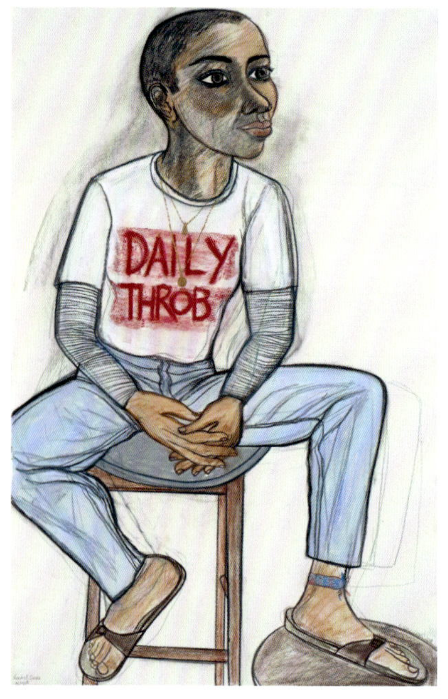

v

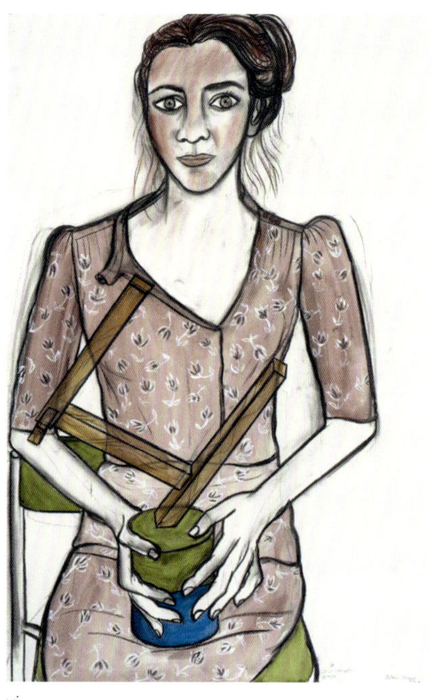

vi

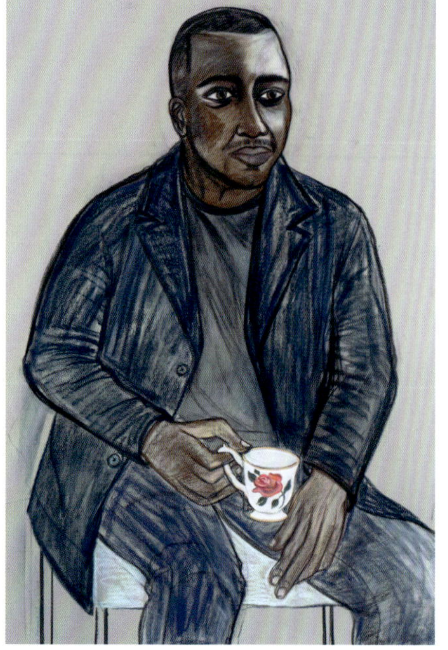

vii

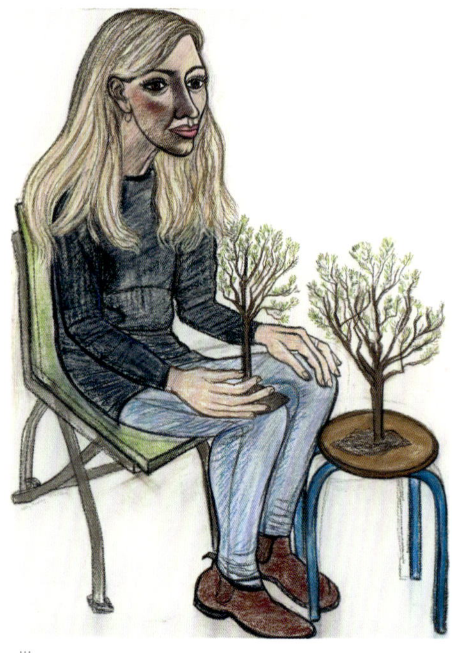

viii

v *Portrait of Rachel Jones*, 2019, charcoal and pastel on paper, 101.5 × 66 cm
vi *Coco Crampton*, 2018, charcoal, pastel and watercolour on paper, 101.5 × 66 cm
vii *Olu Ogunnaike*, 2018, charcoal and pastel on paper, 115.5 × 75.5cm
viii *Suzanne Moxhay*, 2019, charcoal and pastel on paper, 106 × 75.5 cm

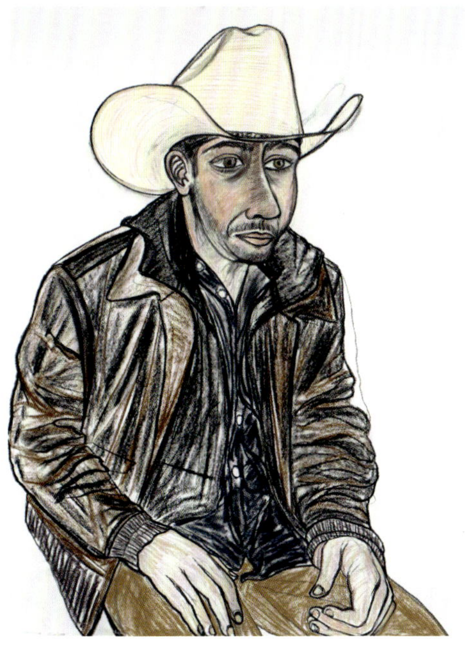

ix

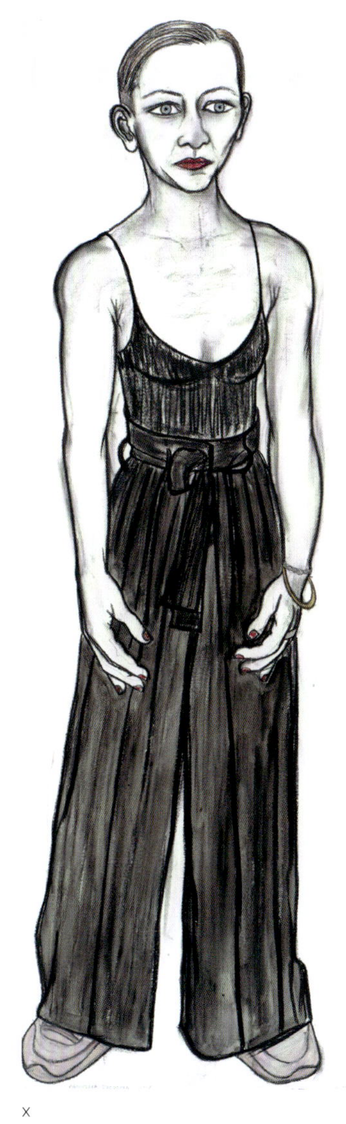
x

ix *Dmitri Galitzine*, 2019, charcoal and pastel on paper, 119 × 89.5 cm
x *Agnieszka Szczotka*, 2018, charcoal and pastel on paper, 154 × 53.5 cm

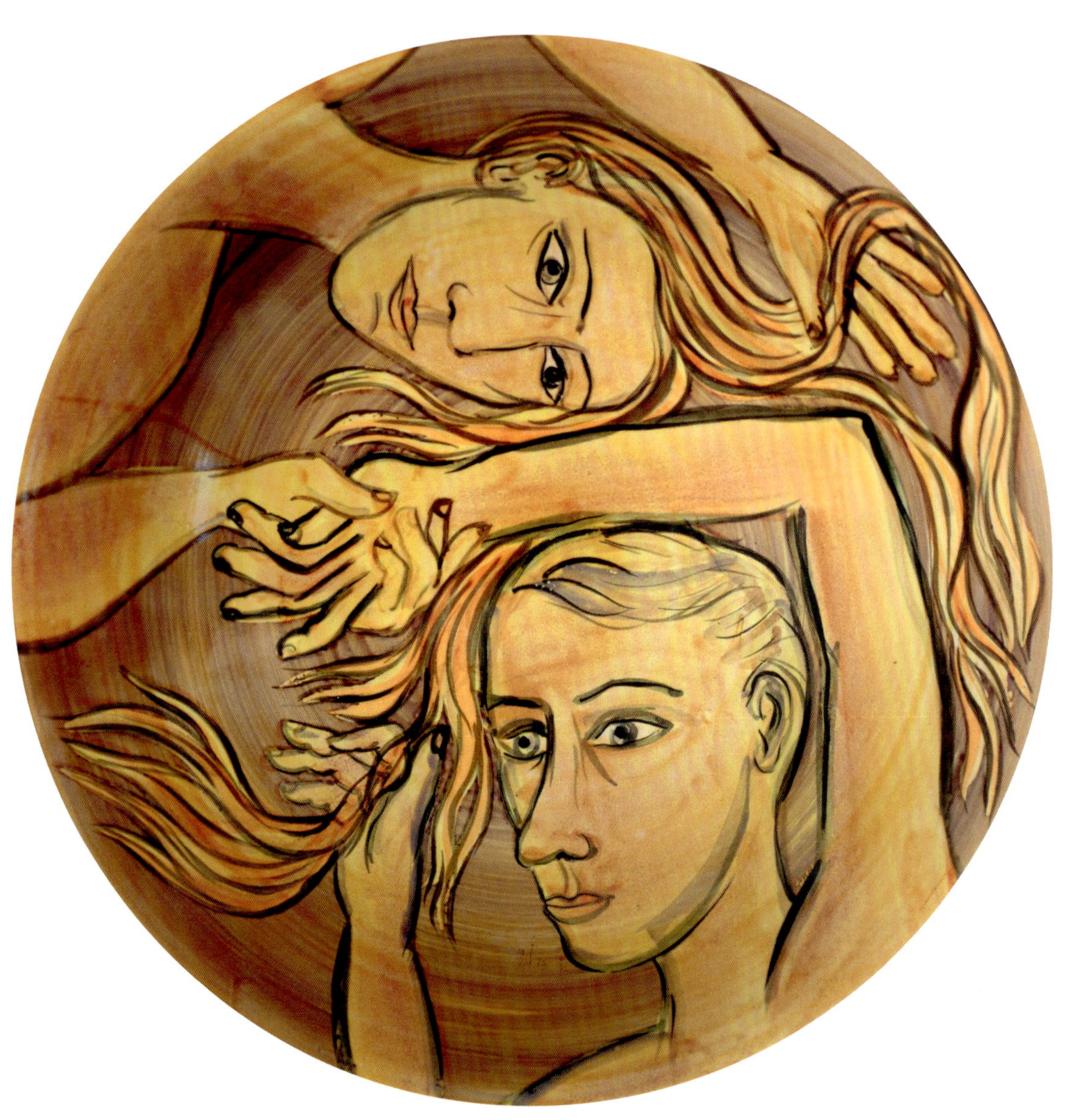

Detail: *Tangled* (p. 80)

4 CERAMICS

In the same way that Cooper is drawn to printmaking because it is a collaborative process involving a number of people, her interest in ceramics grew out of a relationship with the women artists Janice Tchalenko, Glenys Barton and Jacqui Poncelet when they were all teaching at Camberwell School of Art. Later, Eileen Cooper shared a ceramics studio with sculptor Annie Turner who mentored and assisted her in the development of her own work in the medium. Working together, Turner and Cooper secured a grant to create an exhibition of their ceramics in Midlands Arts Centre, Birmingham in 2000.

In 2018 Leicester Museum acquired a large body of Pablo Picasso designed ceramics, donated by Lord and Lady Attenborough and collected by them when visiting the Madoura pottery in Vallauris, France in the 1950s and 1960s. Picasso remains one of the most prolific and influential artists of the 20th century. Founder of Cubism his work ranged across media including drawing, printmaking, painting and sculpture, only coming to ceramics in his sixties. Between 1947 and 1971 he designed over 3,500 ceramics, beginning with decorated utilitarian objects such as plates and bowls, where he experimented with different techniques, going on to produce more complex forms such as pitchers and vases.

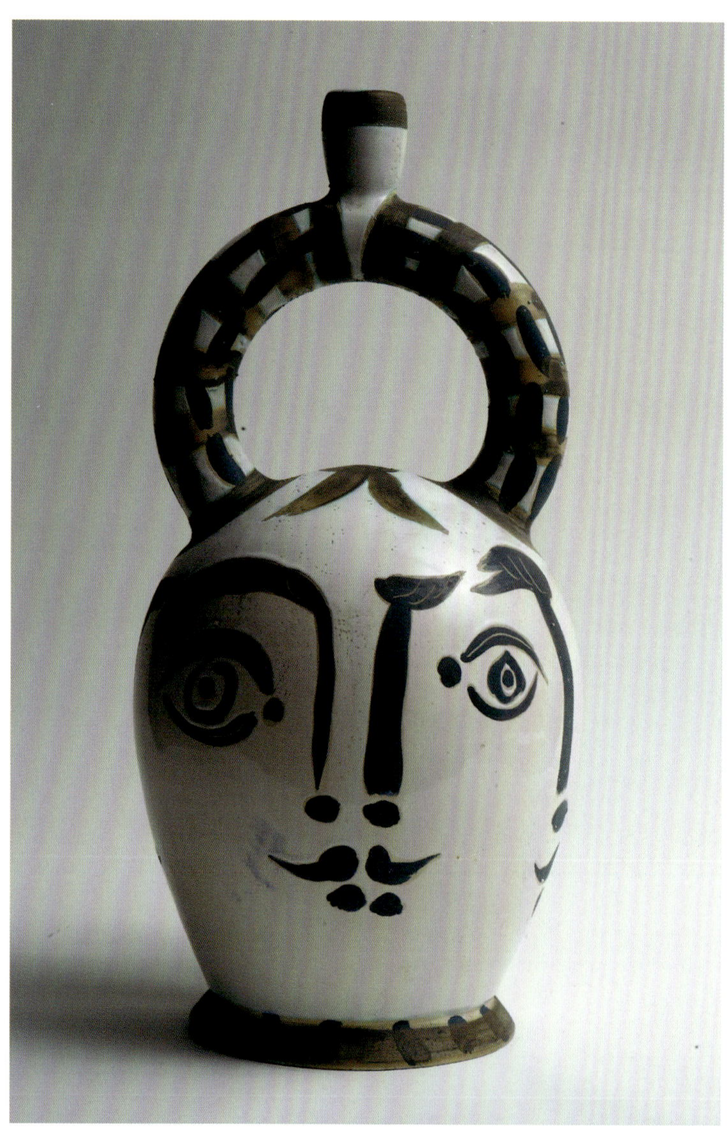

PABLO PICASSO
(1881–1973)

33
Heads of Women 1957 (design by Picasso)
Earthenware, 51 × 26 × 26 cm

Leicester Museums & Galleries: From the collection of Lord and Lady Attenborough. Accepted in lieu by HM Government in 2018 and allocated to Leicester City Council

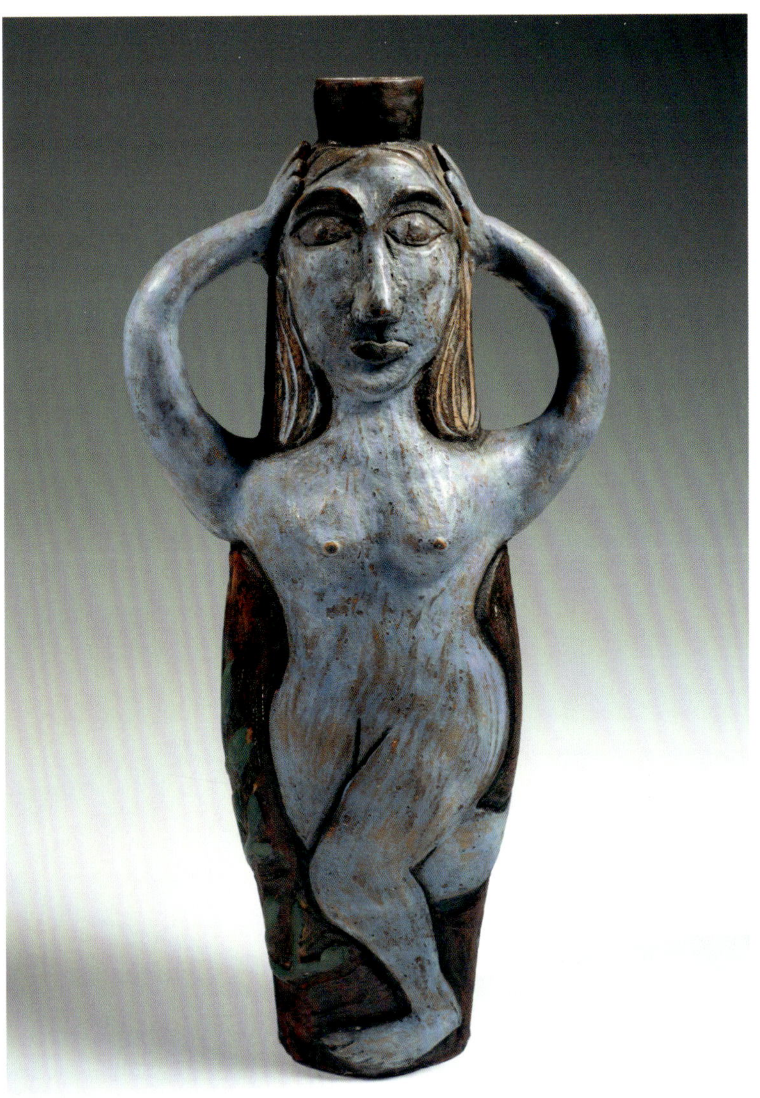

34
Witness II 1999
Handbuilt red clay with slip, 52 × 25 × 15 cm

Eileen Cooper Family Collection

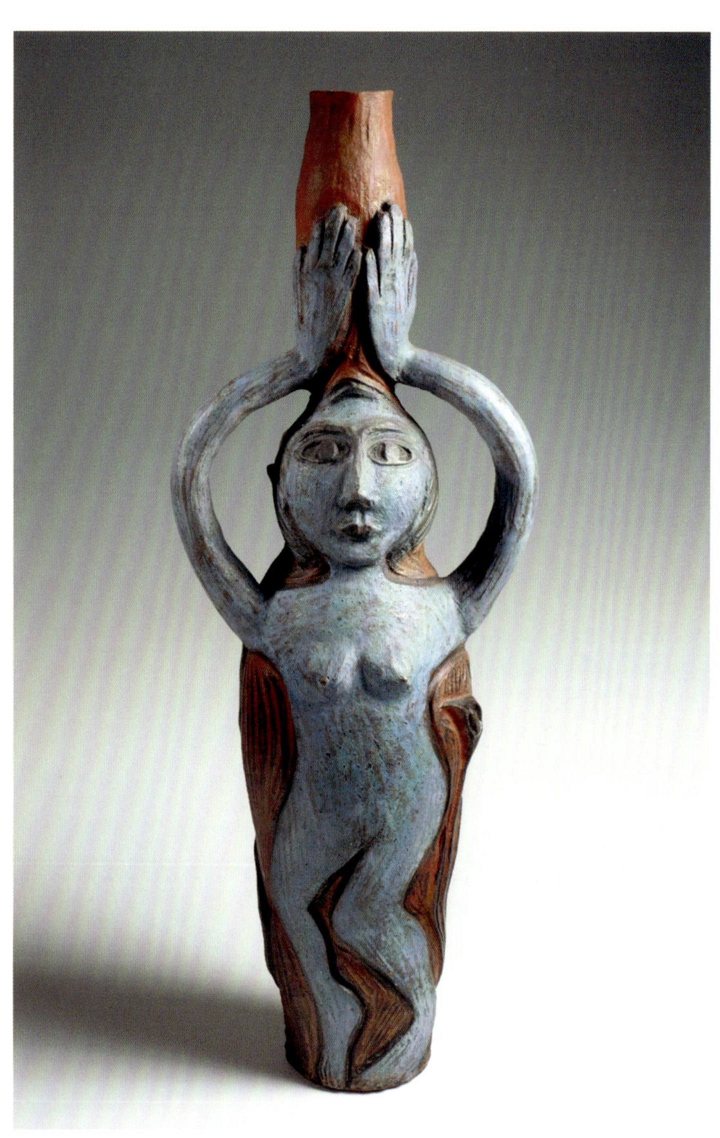

35
Witness I 1999
Handbuilt, red clay with slip, 77 × 28 × 20 cm

Eileen Cooper Family Collection

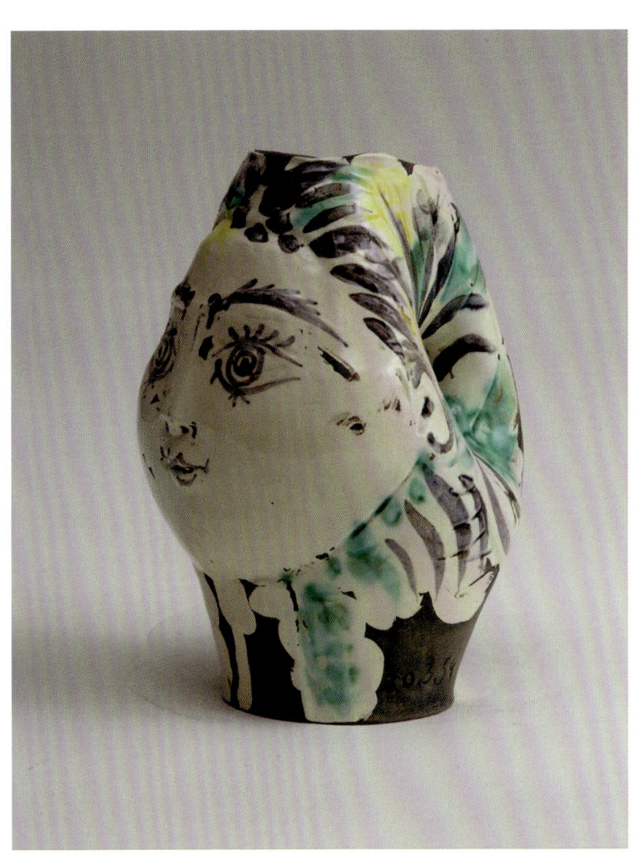

PABLO PICASSO
(1881–1973)

36
Head of a Woman 1954 (design by Picasso)
Earthenware, 22.5 × 16 × 16 cm

Leicester Museums & Galleries: From the collection of Lord and Lady Attenborough. Accepted in lieu by HM Government in 2018 and allocated to Leicester City Council

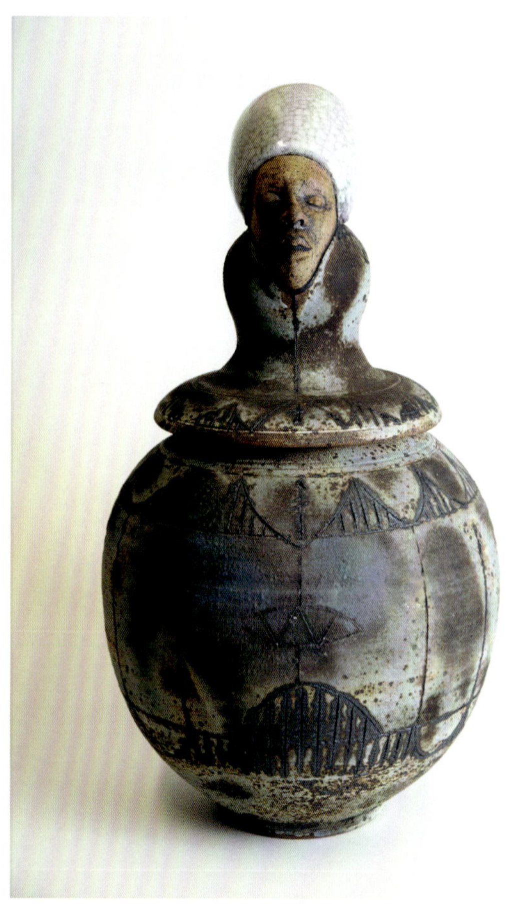

CHRIS BRAMBLE
(b. 1958)

37
The Young Prince c.1993
Ceramic, stoneware, raku glaze
Lid: 21 cm (height), 18 cm (diameter)
Vase: 25 cm (height), 23 cm (diameter)

Leicester Museums & Galleries: Purchased from the City Gallery with financial assistance from East Midlands Arts, 1994

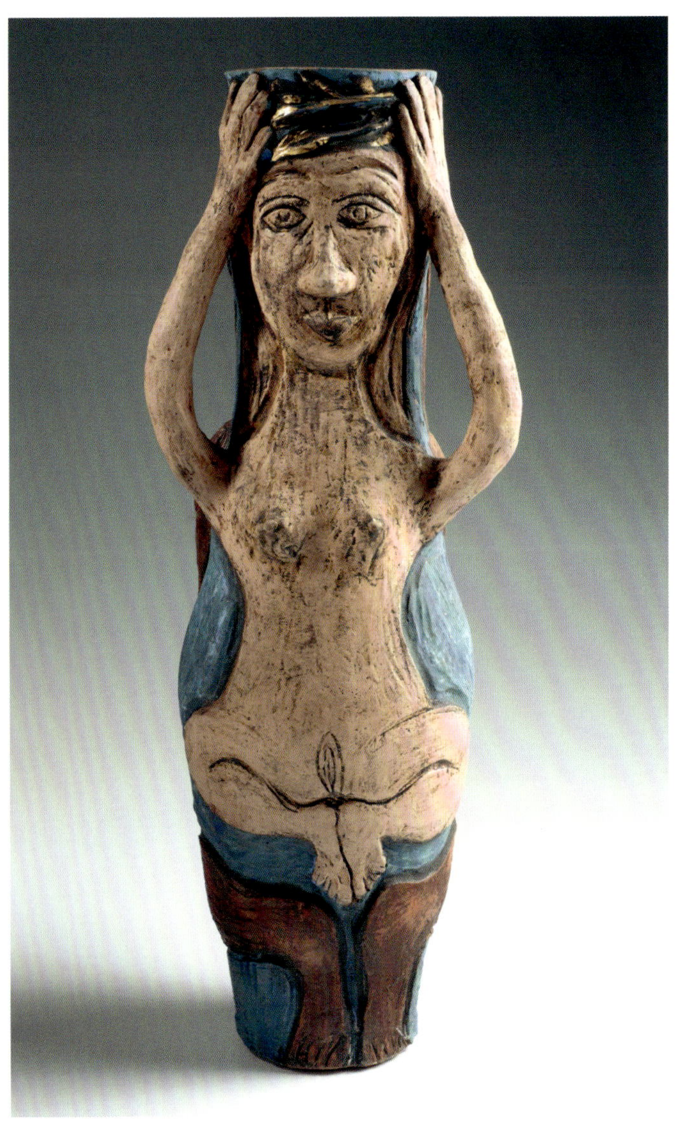

38
Witness III 1999
Handbuilt, red clay with slip, 54 × 17 × 16 cm

Eileen Cooper Family Collection

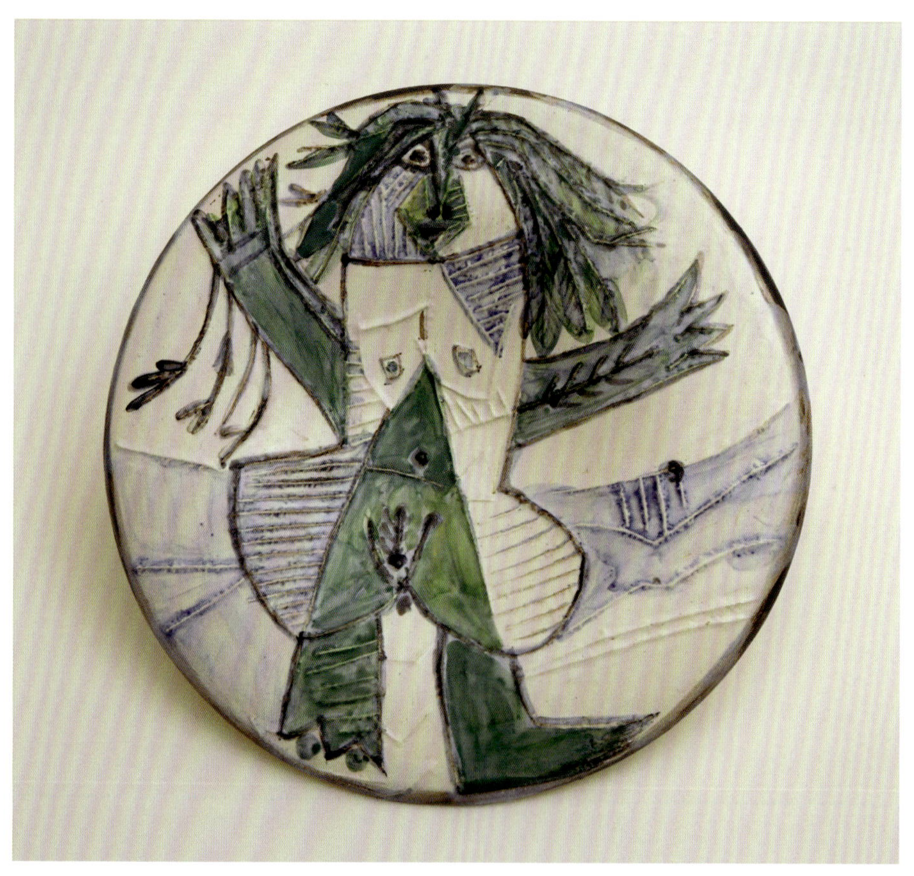

PABLO PICASSO
(1881–1973)

39
Female Nude at the Beach 1963 (design by Picasso)
White earthenware, decorated with slips,
27 cm (diameter)

Leicester Museums & Galleries: From the collection of Lord and Lady Attenborough. Accepted in lieu by HM Government in 2018 and allocated to Leicester City Council

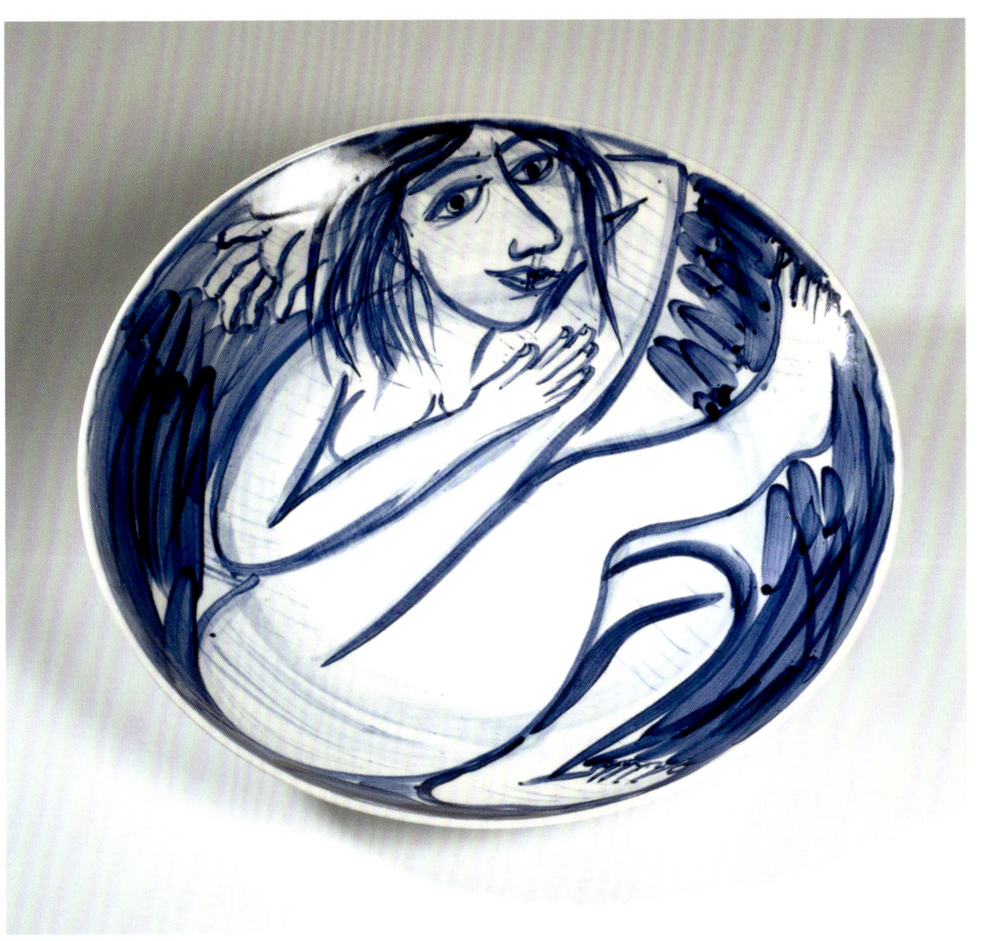

EILEEN COOPER and JULIAN STAIR

40
Sitting Pretty 1999
Porcelain, 40 cm (diameter)

Eileen Cooper Family Collection

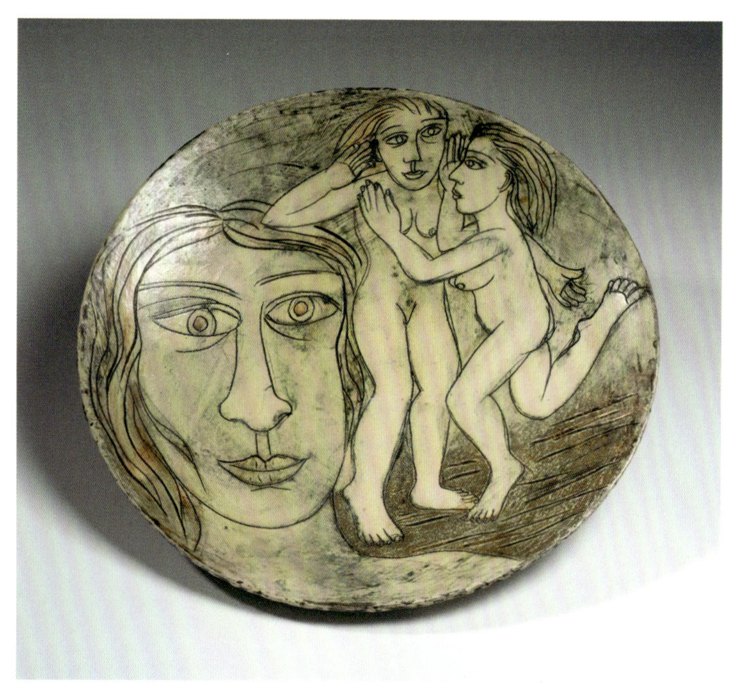

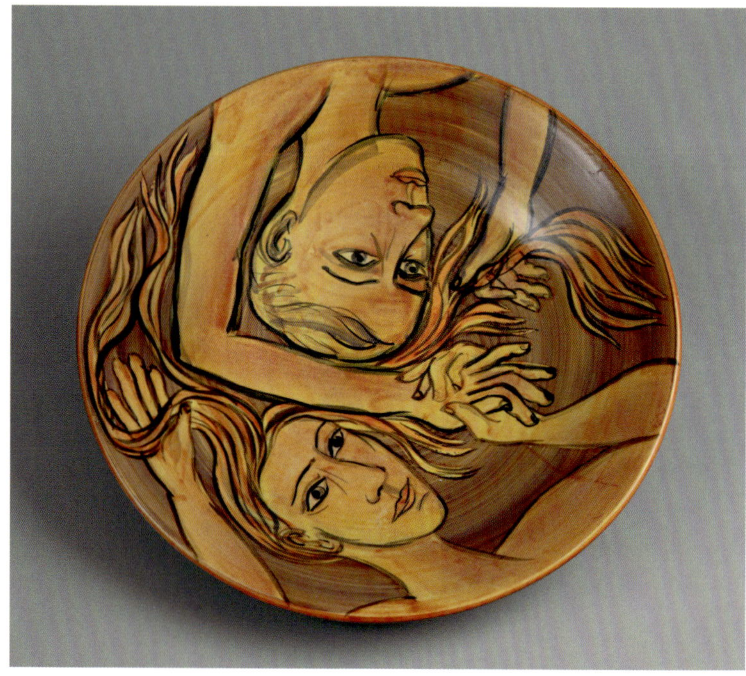

41
Memory Plate 2000
Glazed earthenware, 39.5 cm (diameter)

Eileen Cooper Family Collection

42
Tangled 2019
Earthenware, 34 cm (diameter)

Eileen Cooper Family Collection

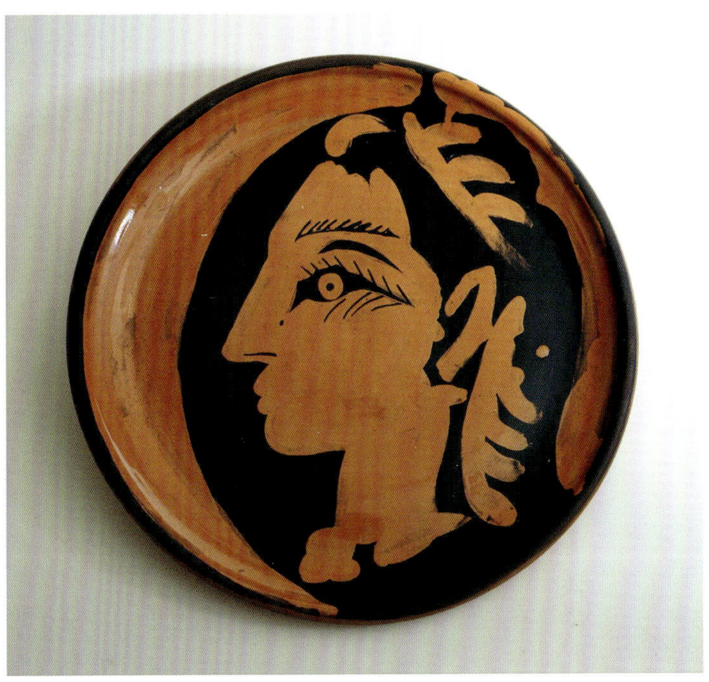

PABLO PICASSO
(1881–1973)

43
Profile of Jacqueline 1962 (design by Picasso)
Red earthenware, decorated with glaze,
35.5 cm (diameter)

Leicester Museums & Galleries: From the collection of Lord and Lady Attenborough. Accepted in lieu by HM Government in 2018 and allocated to Leicester City Council

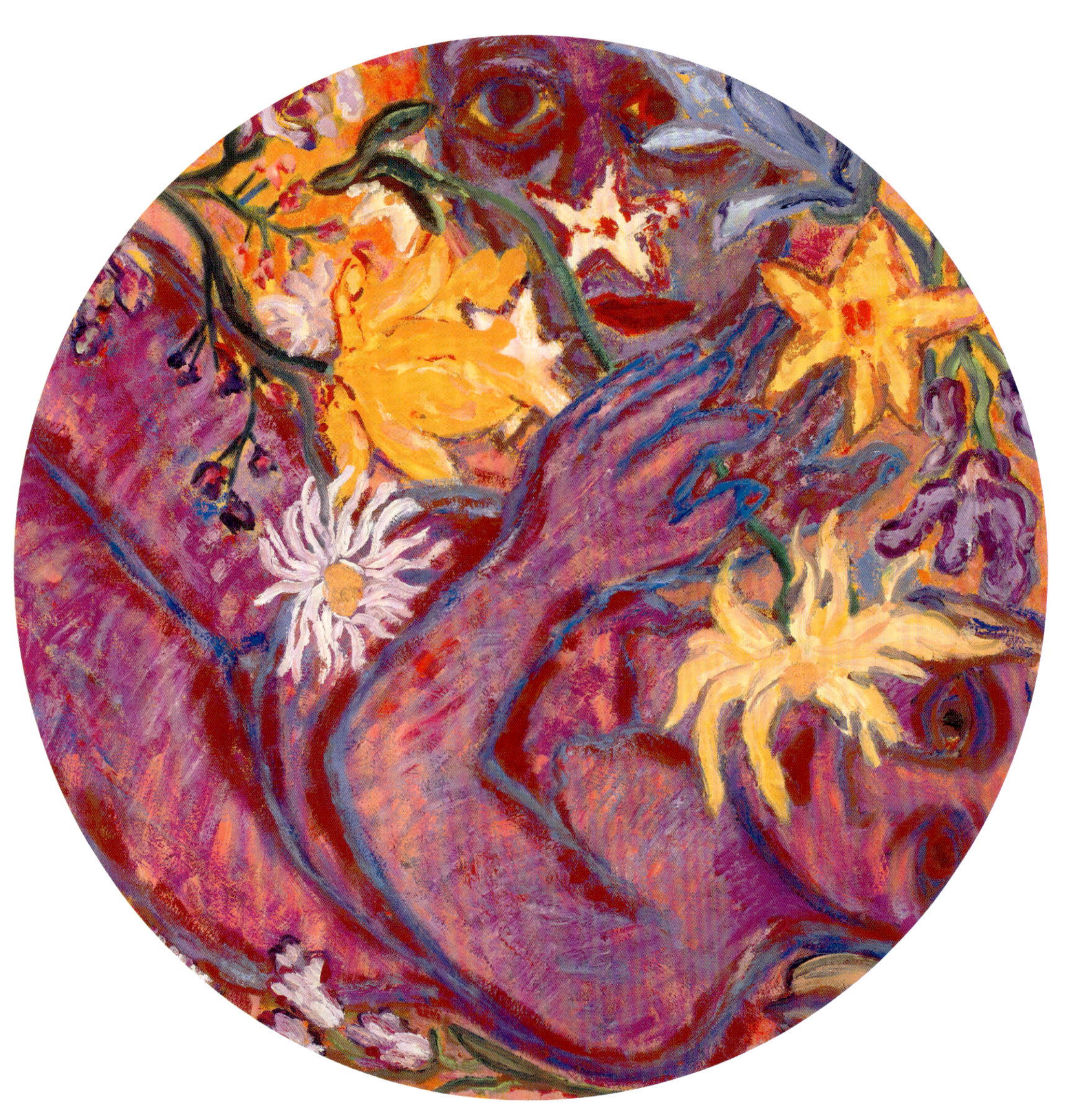

Detail: *One to One* (p. 85)

5 THE NUDE

In 1989, an art critic described Cooper as Britain's new young nudist superstar, given the proliferation of naked figures in her work. However, Cooper doesn't see her figures as naked but, as she puts it, 'beautifully free of clothes'. For her, that nakedness brings us closer to nature, to our fundamental selves, and allows her to treat the figures as universal, representing us all. Being unclothed gives her figures a primal quality so that we are back at the beginning of time. Cooper has been far more interested in 'clothing' the body in colour than in dresses or t-shirts, with all the signals that they would give off, however her figures have become increasingly clothed as she has grown older.

Naked depictions of men are to be found in early Classical sculpture, often reflecting the sporting prowess of Olympian athletes or conquering heroes. Women however were already present in their naked form in early pre-historic sculpture, associated with procreation and fertility. Early paintings of the female nude took inspiration from the Bible or mythology, and in the 18th and 19th centuries artists, almost exclusively male, were still interested in the allegorical nude but also began painting real women in their day-to-day environments. While the male gaze meant that these nudes were often depicted as objects of desire, today the naked female body is politically charged, and very much reclaimed by women artists.

Cooper's nudes are rarely solitary figures. They revel in companionship, wrapped around each other, entwined, supported, loved.

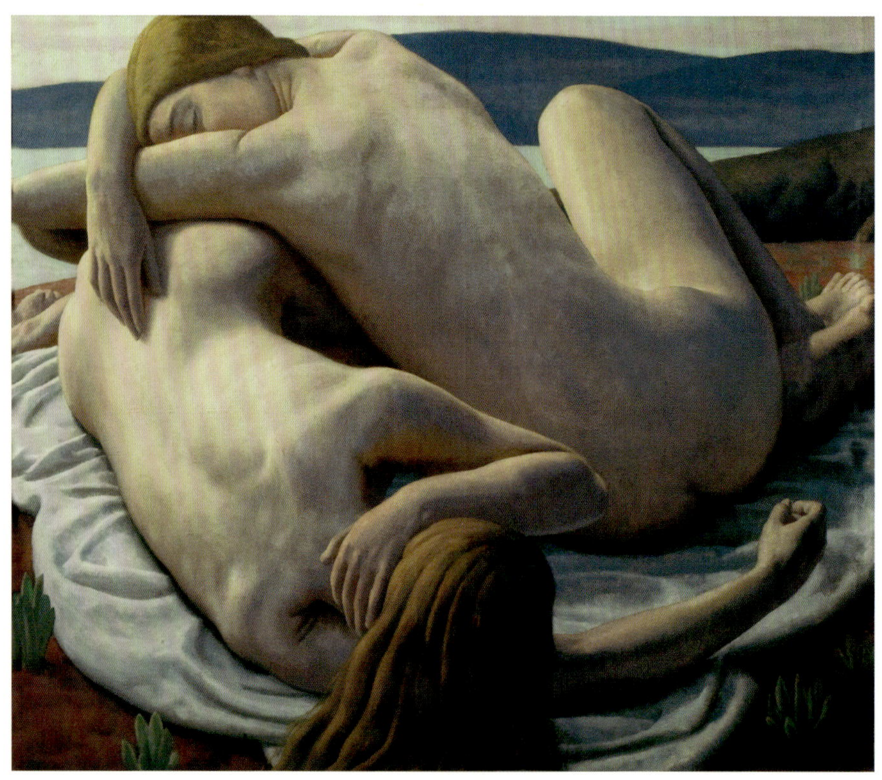

ERNEST PROCTER
(1885–1935)

44
The Day's End 1927
Oil on canvas, 91.5 × 106.5 cm

Leicester Museums & Galleries:
Purchased from the artist, 1928

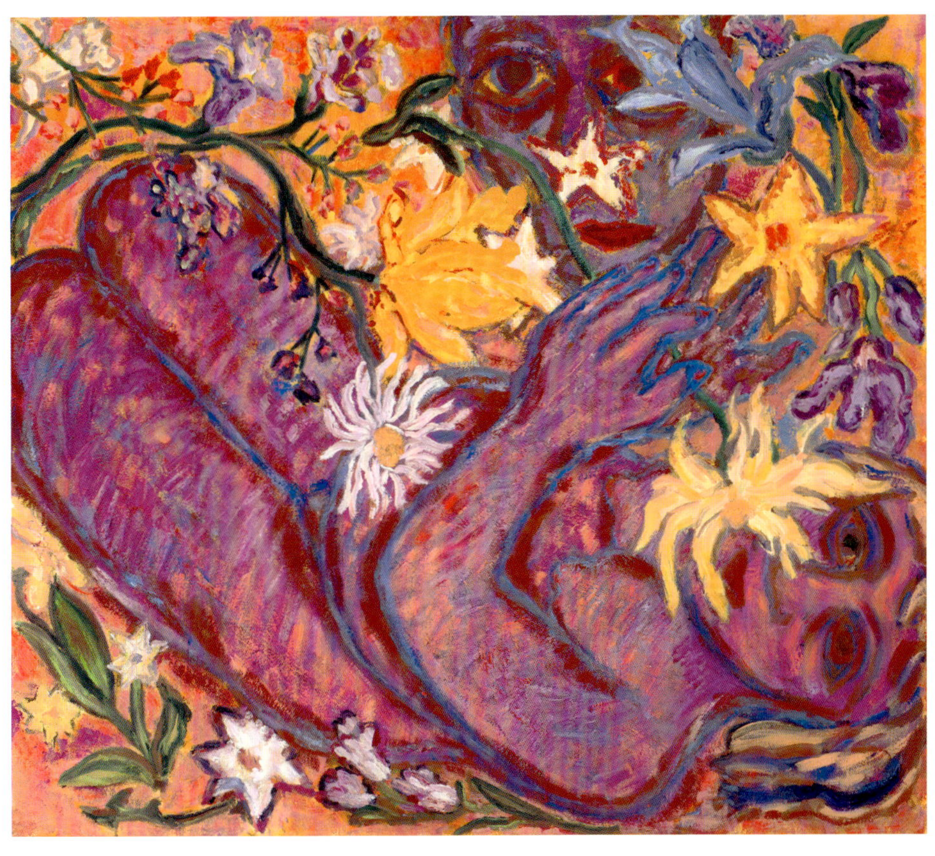

45
One to One 1986
Oil on canvas, 107 × 123 cm

Private Collection

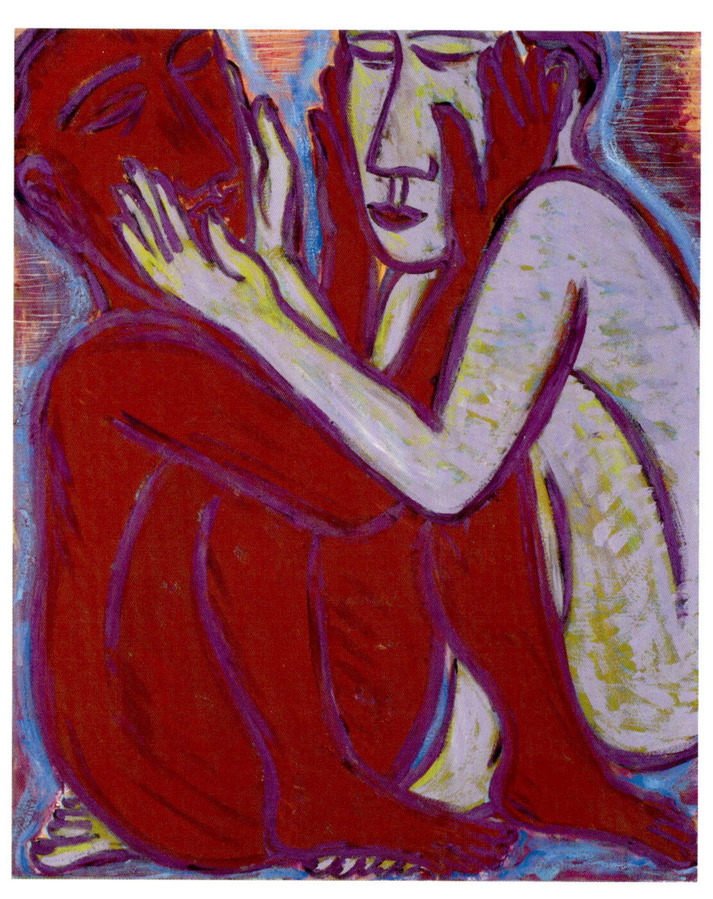

46
Communion 1998
Oil on canvas, 92 × 76.5 cm

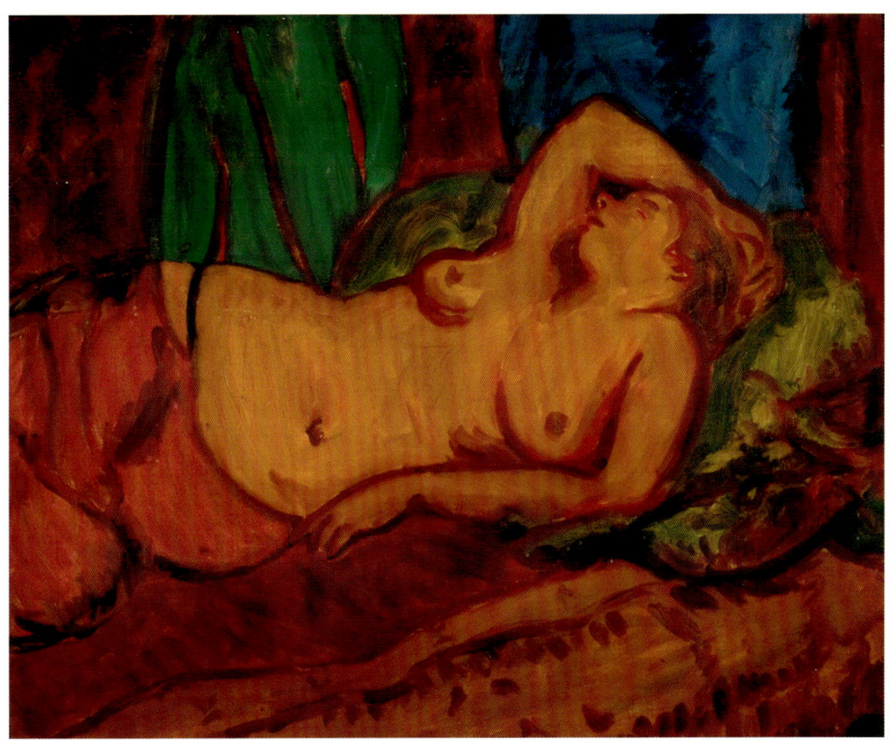

MATTHEW SMITH
(1879–1959)

47
Reclining Nude 1924
Oil on canvas, 66 × 82 cm

Leicester Museums & Galleries:
Purchased from Arthur Tooth and Sons, 1948

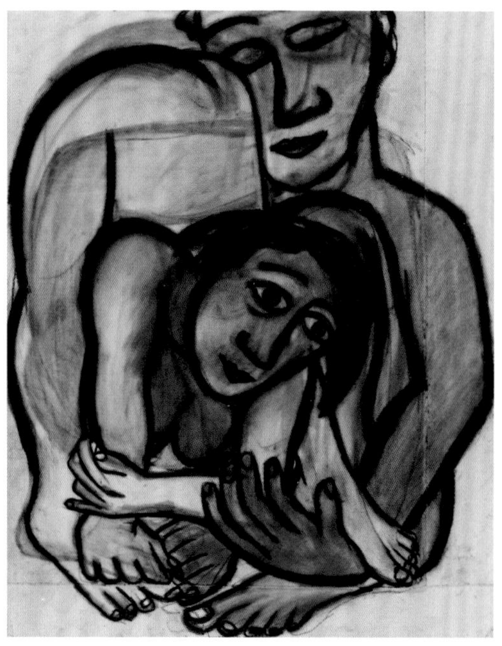

i

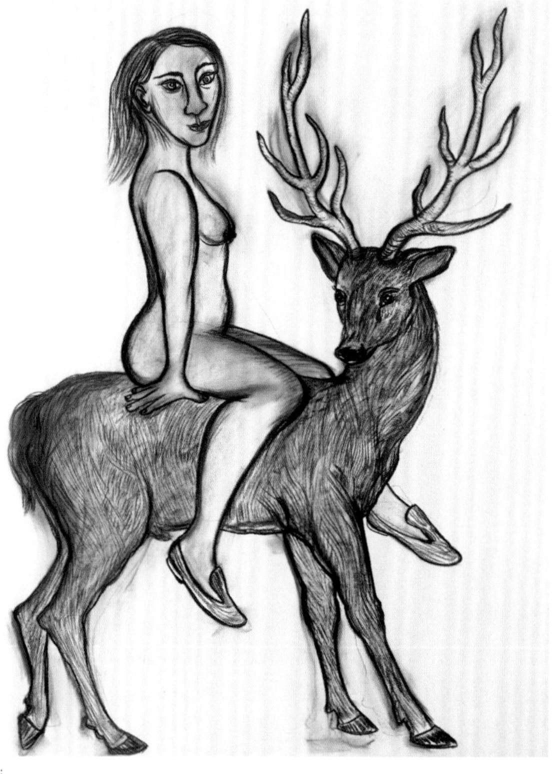

ii

i *Remembrance*, 1989, charcoal on paper 83.2 × 66.7 cm (Private Collection)
ii *Demeter*, 2014, charcoal on paper 120 × 90 cm
iii *Freefall*, 2000, oil on canvas, 122.5 × 122.5 cm
iv *Ritual*, 2019, oil on canvas, 92 × 61 cm (Private Collection)
v *Warm Water*, 2018, oil on canvas, 90 × 60 cm (Private Collection)

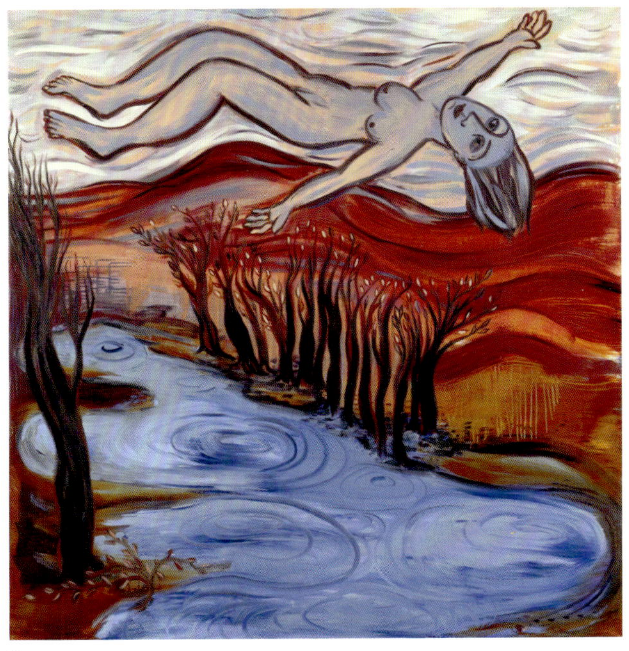
iii

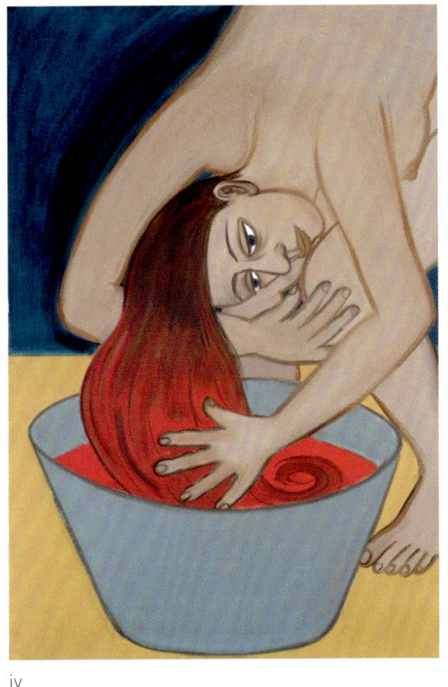
iv

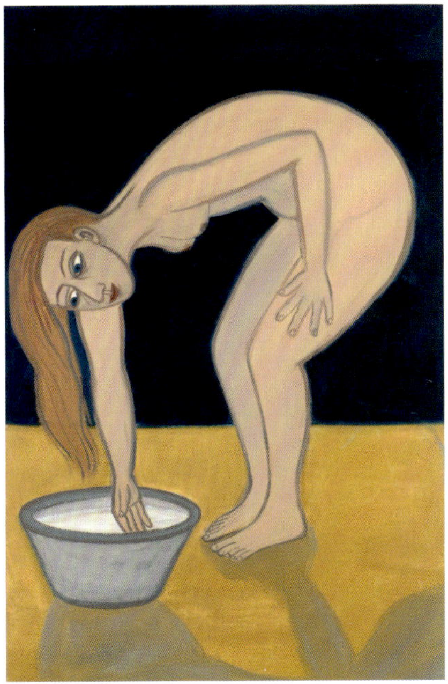
v

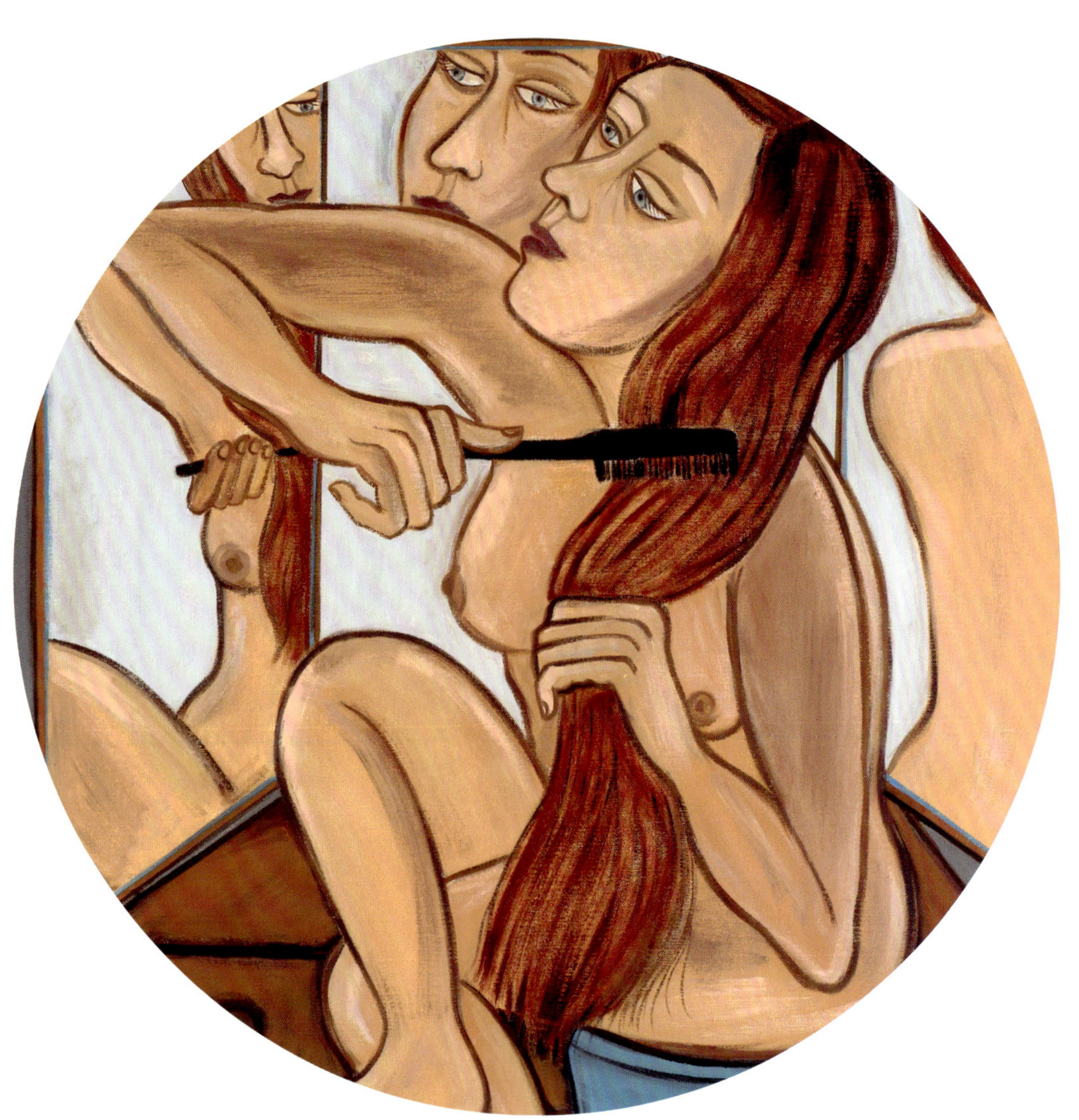

Detail: *Personal Space* (p. 94)

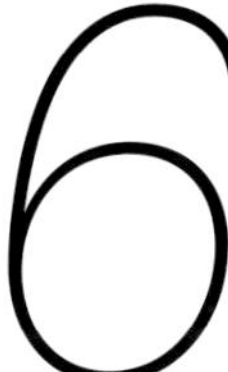

LA TOILETTE

The process of female grooming, its associations with seduction and temptation, has fascinated artists since the Renaissance. Usually taking place behind closed doors, the occupation can suggest hidden arts, artifice, witchcraft even, so that paintings depicting the activity have a voyeuristic air of the male gaze. For women, it is more often about ritual, privacy and friendship, even if with a lady's maid. Often involving the process of bathing, where women are at their most vulnerable, naked, alone, and unaware of being watched, painting in this genre tended to reflect on the fallen woman, prostitutes or mistresses, alternatively an idealised version of a woman. If the main character in the genre is the female, clothed, or unclothed, then the supporting actor is frequently the mirror, reflecting our true selves back at us.

In Cooper's paintings these are intimate moments of self-absorption and respite, private though companionable. She observes the rhythms and rituals of preparing oneself to face the world, her characters quietly confident and knowing, a place where women work together in support of each other.

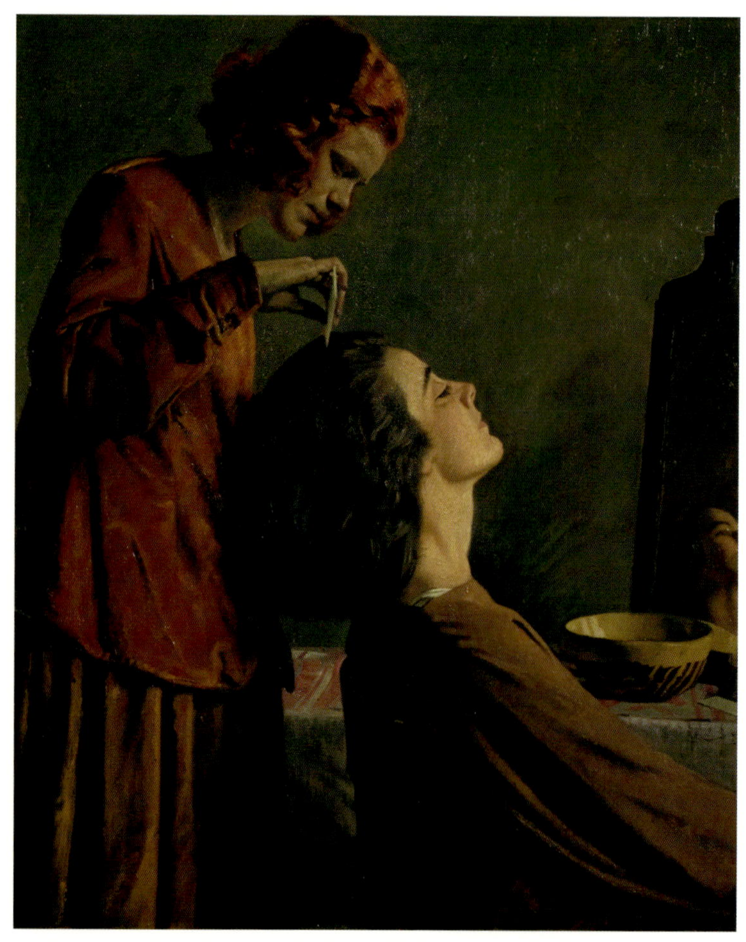

WILLIAM ROTHENSTEIN
(1872–1945)

48
The Toilet 1924
Oil on canvas, 91.5 × 76.4 cm

Leicester Museums & Galleries: Purchased from the artist via the Goupil Gallery, 1931

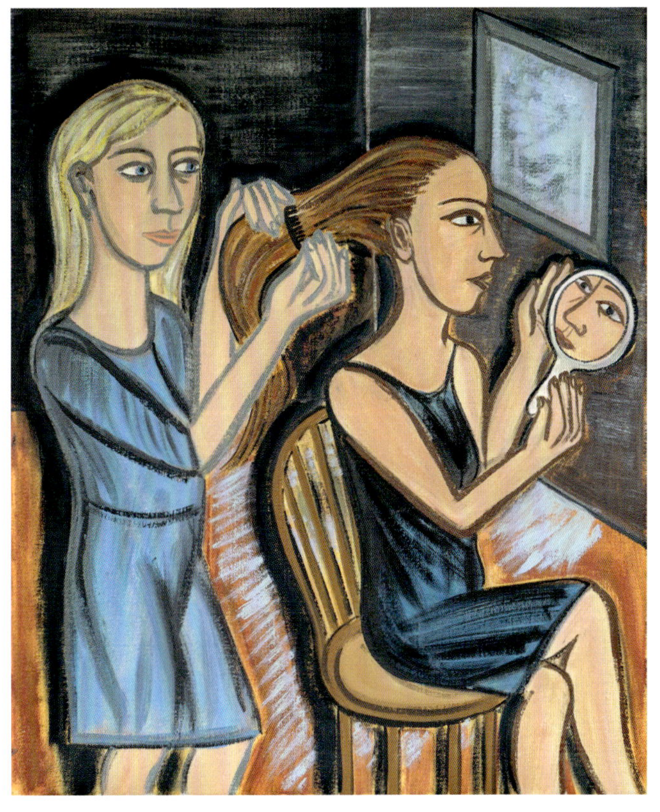

49
A Special Kind of Double 2020
Oil on canvas, 61 × 51 cm

Private Collection

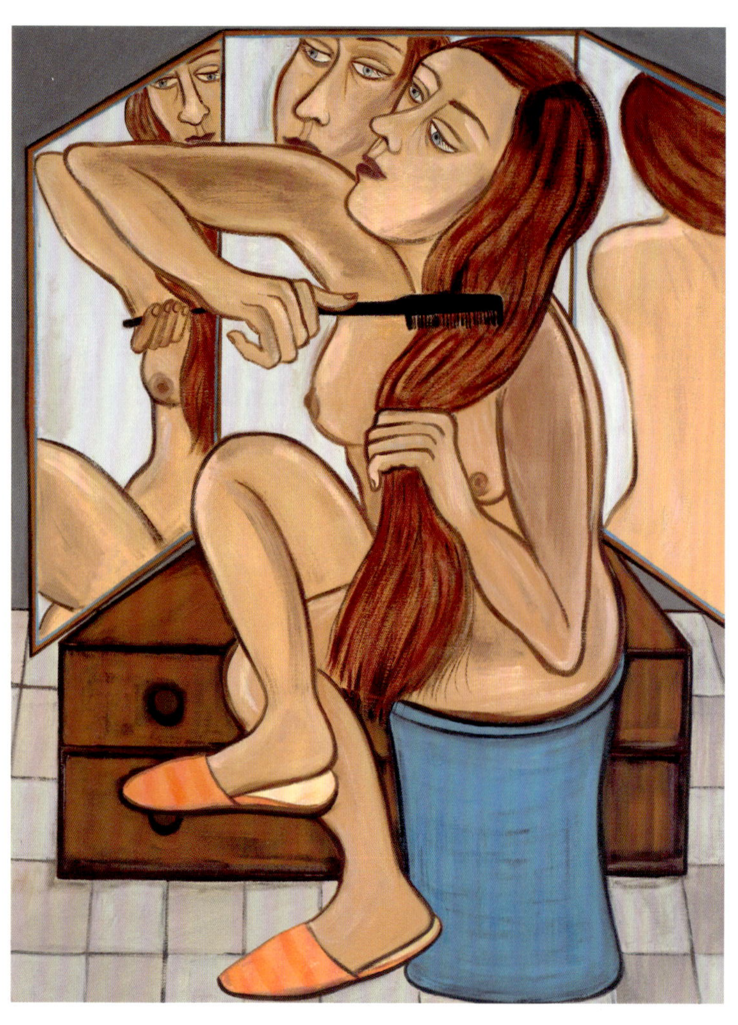

50
Personal Space 2019
Oil on canvas, 122 × 92 cm

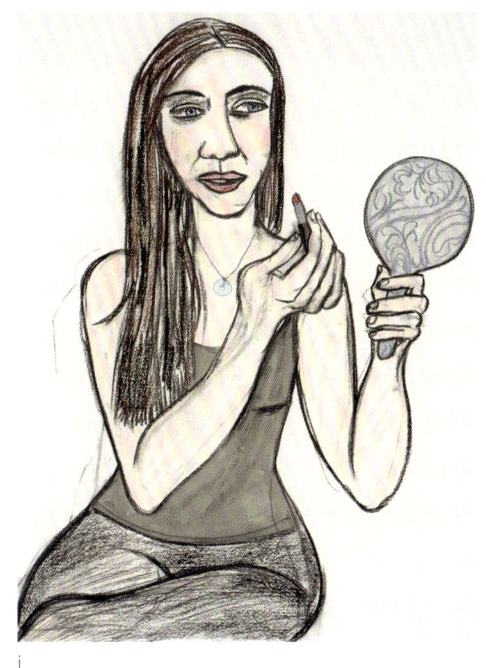

i

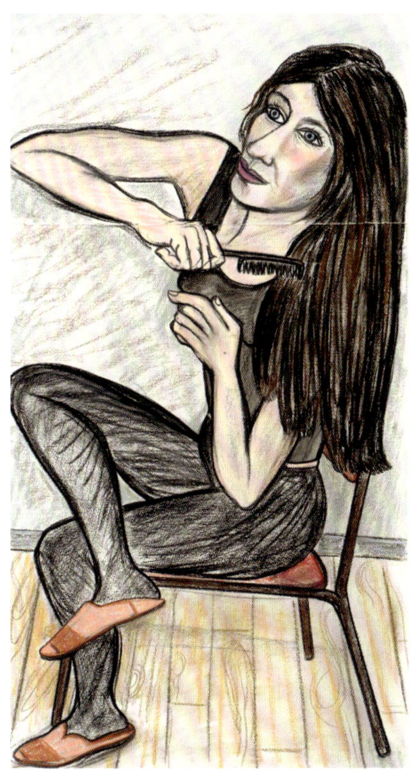

ii

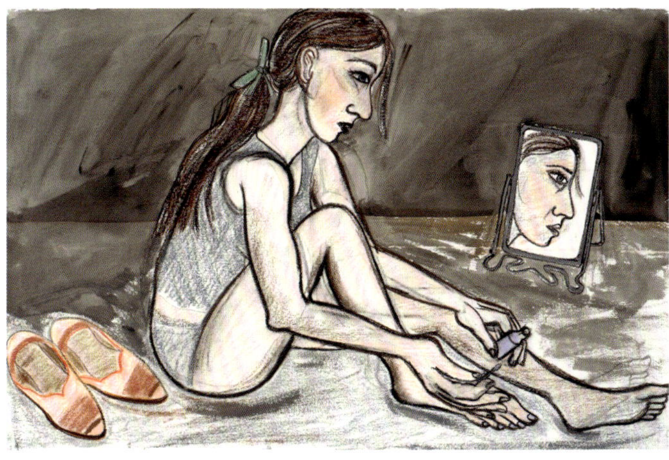

iii

i *Lipstick*, 2019, charcoal and pastel on paper, 76 × 56 cm
ii *Combing Hair*, 2019, charcoal and pastel on paper, 106 × 56 cm
iii *Painting Nails*, 2019, charcoal and pastel on paper, 66 × 102 cm (Private Collection)

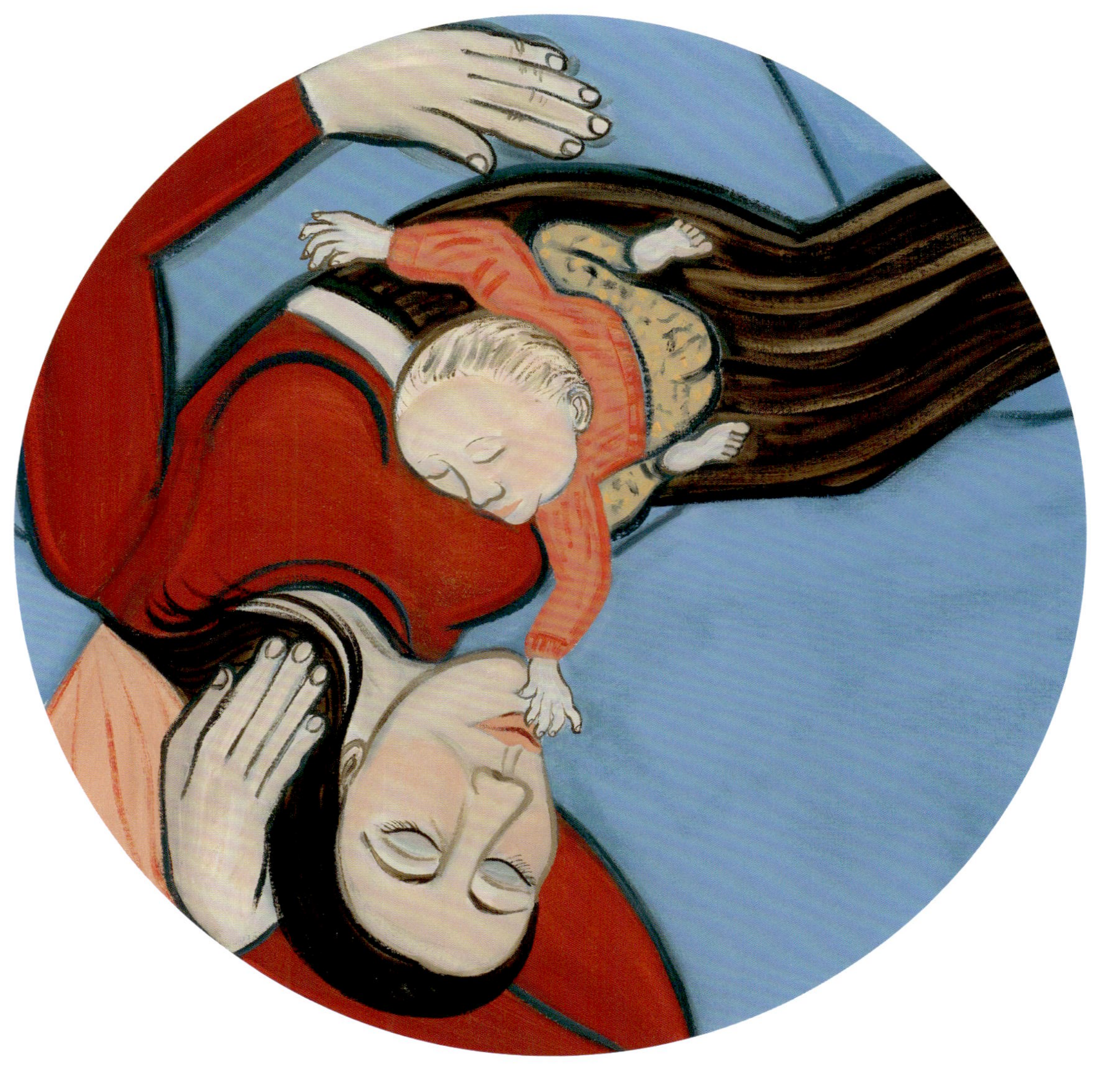

Detail: *Mother's Day* (p. 101)

7 MOTHER AND CHILD

The autobiographical nature of Cooper's work, that sees her respond to what is in front of her, embraced the arrival of her two sons in the mid-1980s. Coming to believe that creativity was closely associated with nurture, she found herself drawing about the experiences of motherhood. Her sons went on to populate her paintings, but rarely as the adults that they had become, until the arrival of her first grandchild, recently depicted with her father, Cooper's adult son. The arrival of a granddaughter has resulted in a revisiting of motherhood for Cooper. This time she has been able to approach it with a cooler, more objective view where she can observe rather than, as she puts it, feeling it from the inside out.

The popularity of the theme of mother and child in art, at least in the Western tradition, goes back to early representations of the Virgin Mary and Baby Jesus, where the Christ child was often depicted as a small adult. Realism only became a concern in the Renaissance when artists were more interested in anatomy and true to life representations.

After a brief period of unpopularity, the mother and child came to the fore again with the Impressionists who largely transformed the idealised depiction of the Virgin and Child into flesh and blood. Their interest was in tenderness, the warmth of relationship and the intimate bond. However, while many artists were producing romantic visions of motherhood others, such as the German artist Käthe Kollwitz, were examining the complexities and emotions of parenting in the war-torn world of the early 20th century.

In Cooper's depictions of motherhood there is an exploration of the personal, with her own children often shown with birds representing a freedom of spirit. The raw, visceral nature of the works indicate her natural interest in the physical body, the idea of the child inhabiting it and the complex, physically reliant and emotional relationship that evolves.

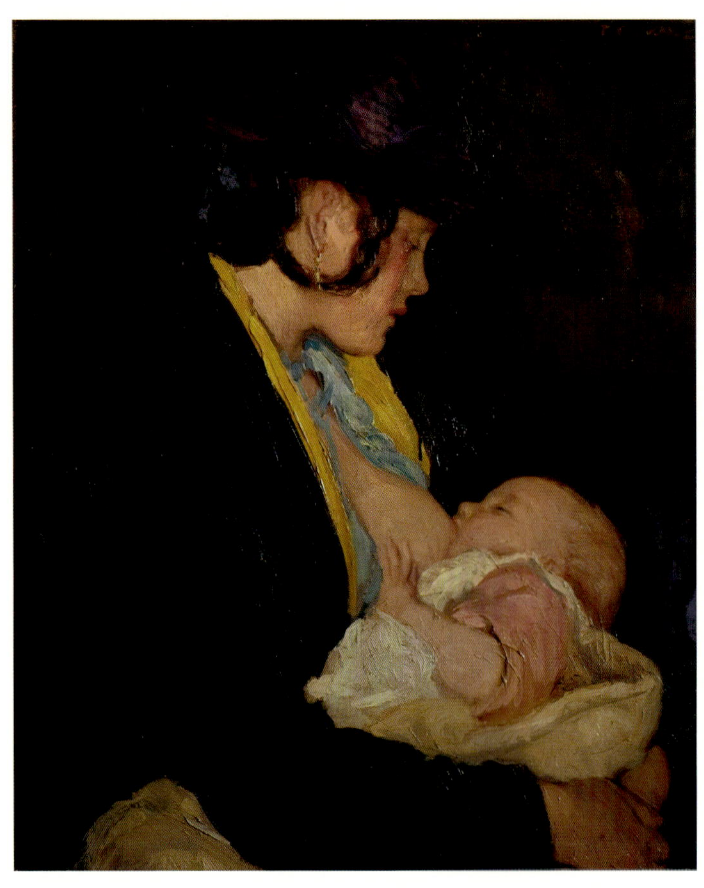

THOMAS CANTRELL DUGDALE
(1880–1952)

51
Motherhood c.1921
Oil on canvas, 75.5 × 62.2 cm

Leicester Museums & Galleries:
Purchased from the artist, 1923

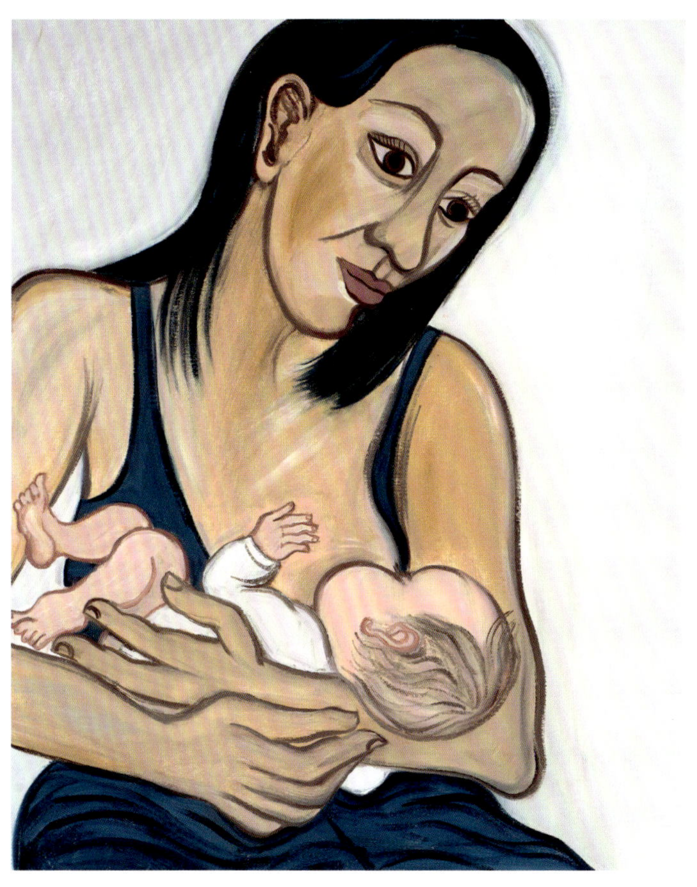

52
Sentimental Mood 2019
Oil on canvas, 76 × 61 cm

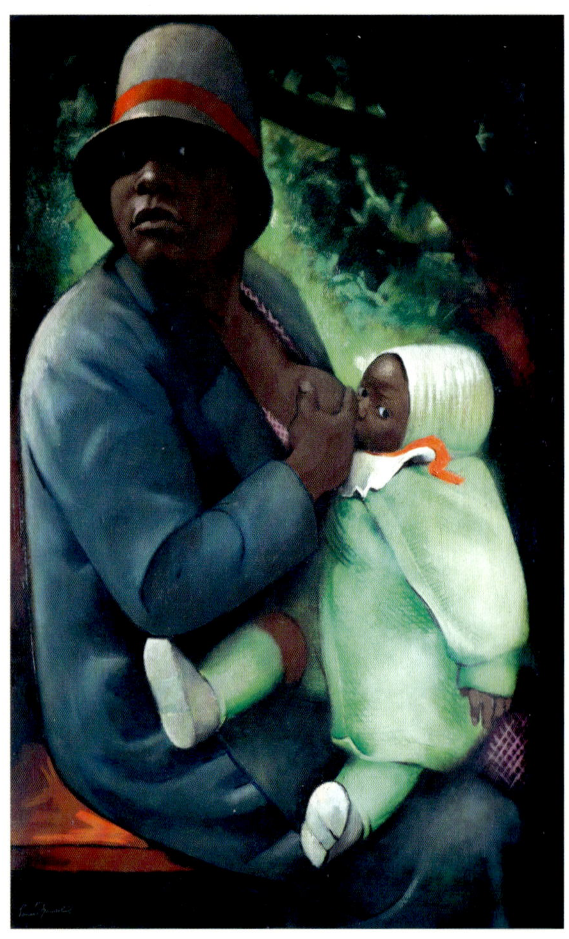

ERNST NEUSCHUL
(1880–1952)

53
Black Mother 1929–31
Oil on canvas, 100.5 × 65.5 cm

Leicester Museums & Galleries: Purchased from Campbell and Franks Ltd with MGC/V&A Purchase Grant Fund assistance, 1978

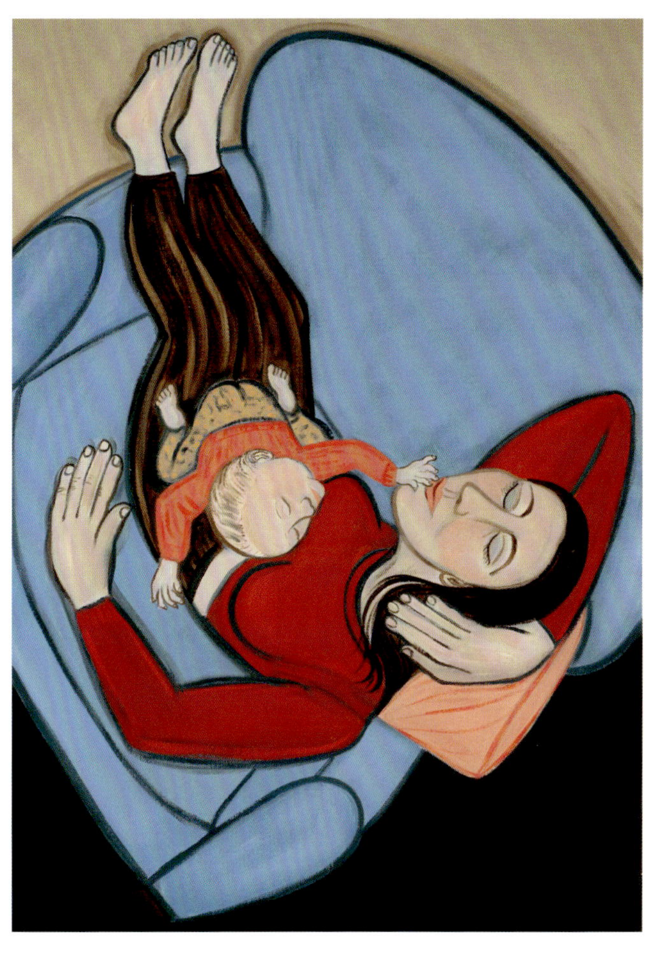

54
Mother's Day 2021
Oil on canvas, 107 × 76 cm

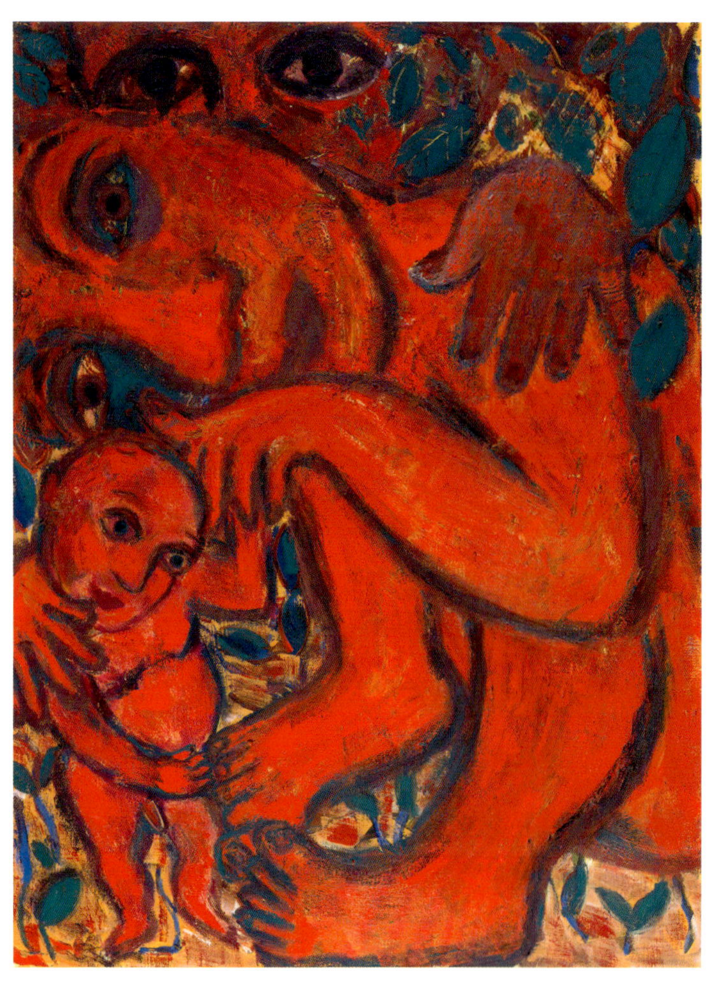

55
Tickling Mummy's Toes 1985
Oil on canvas, 121 × 91 cm

Eileen Cooper Family Collection

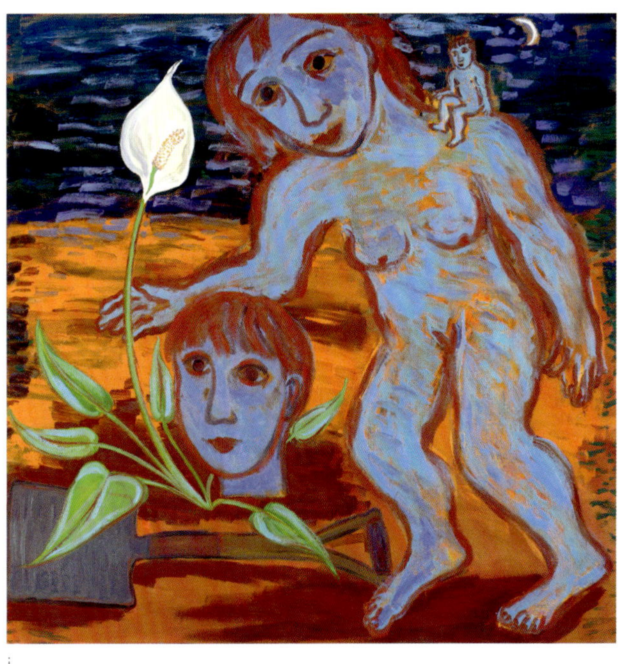

i

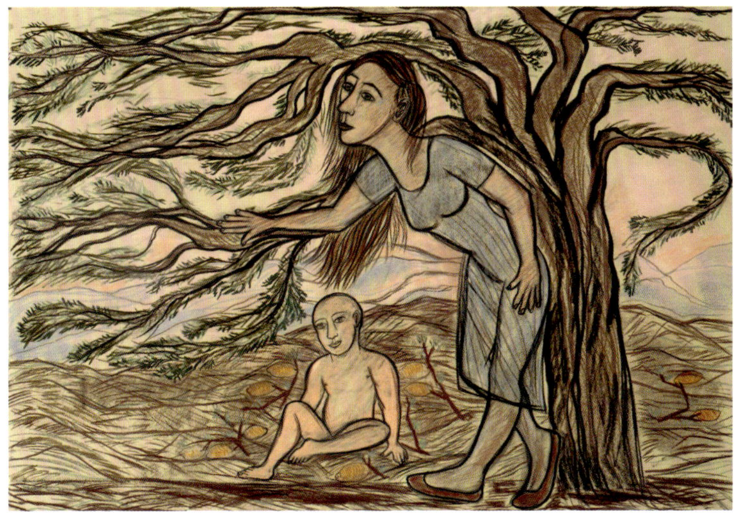

ii

i *Which, What, Why*, 1991, oil on canvas, 122 × 122 cm
ii *Blessing*, 2017, charcoal and pastel on paper, 76.5 × 113 cm

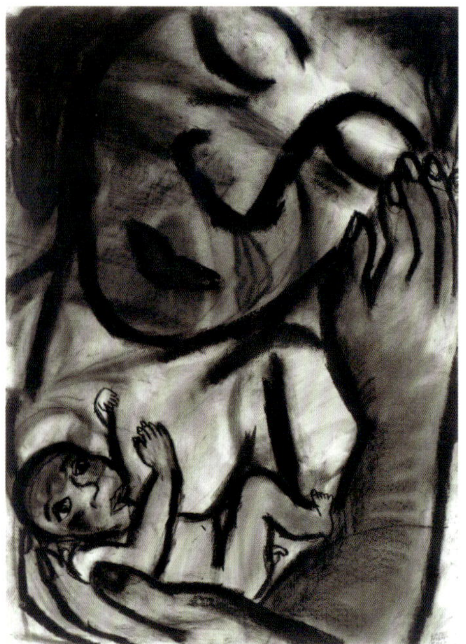

iii

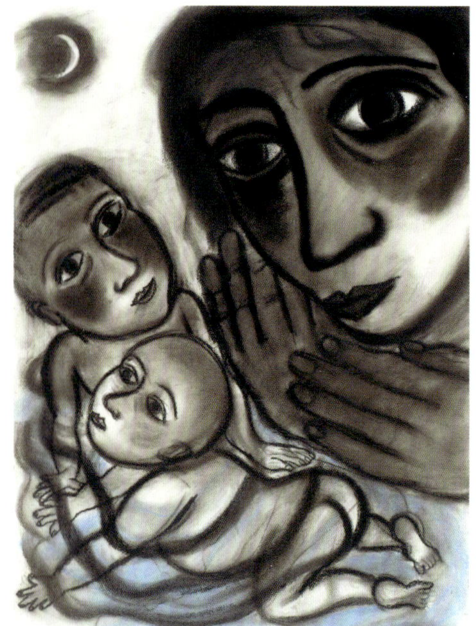

iv

iii *Late Night Feed*, 1985, charcoal on paper, 76 × 56 cm (Eileen Cooper Family Collection)
iv *Bathing*, 1987, charcoal and pastel on paper, 75 × 66 cm (Eileen Cooper Family Collection)
v *The New Baby*, 1988, charcoal on paper, 76 × 55 cm (Eileen Cooper Family Collection)
vi *Father's Day*, 2021, charcoal on paper, 76 × 56 cm (Collection of Alexandra and William Southward)
viii *Pregnant with Twins*, 1999, pastel and Conté on paper, 76 x 56 cm

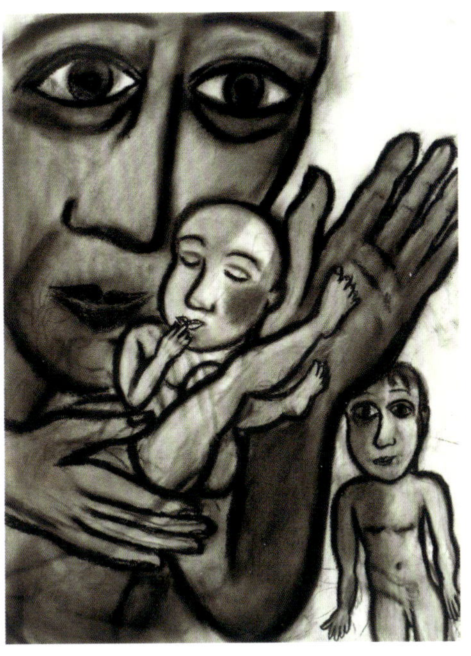

v

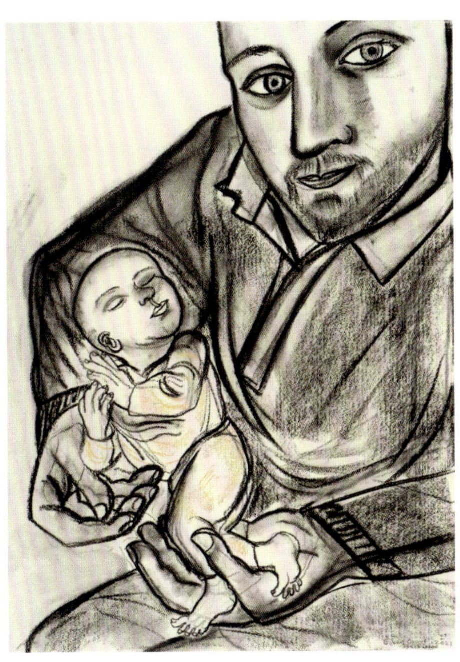

vi

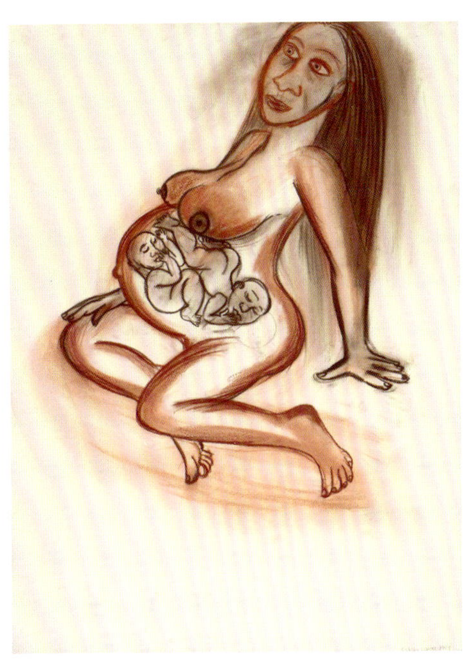

viii

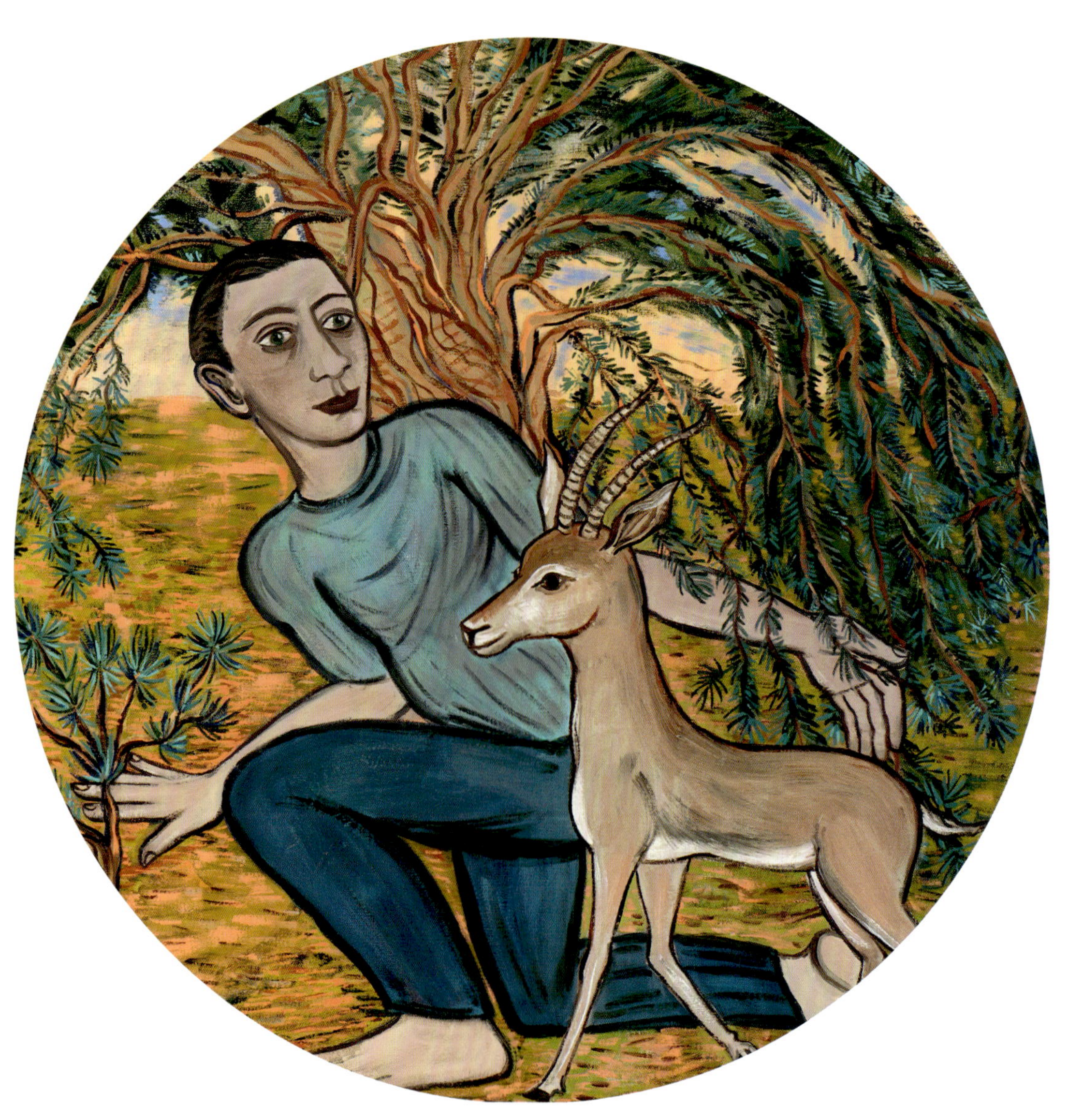

Detail: *Evergreen* (p. 112)

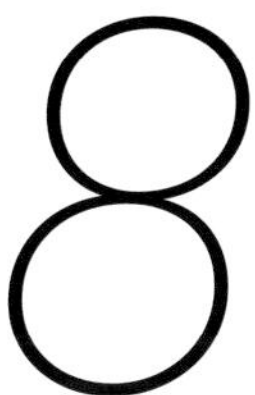

BEASTS

The earliest representations of animals, as a food source but often with spiritual values, are to be found in prehistoric cave art. Later, artists assigned meaning to animals both real and mythological and in Medieval times scholars created bestiaries, illustrated guides describing animals and rocks, supplemented by moral tales associated with specific animals.

Over time, certain animals in art have come to carry commonly recognised meaning, even though that interpretation might have changed over time. Dogs, for example are commonly read as signs of unquestioning loyalty, yet previously their meaning ranged from wisdom to anger, lechery, avarice, and vigilance. The rabbit has long been associated with lust, and monkeys, initially a symbol of the devil, came to be seen as stand-ins for humans – an ape carrying an apple signifying the fall of man for example.

Cooper states that she understands the world through the process of making. She considers the interpretation that the individual viewer brings to her painting the final piece of the jigsaw in completing the work. Like many artists she seeks a reaction, an understanding that gives her work value and meaning to lives other than her own. That response can be complicated by the rich iconography, often animal-related, that populates her work, although she would gently dismiss any request to clarify specific meanings associated with her creatures. These characters frequently re-appear, across the decades, like old friends.

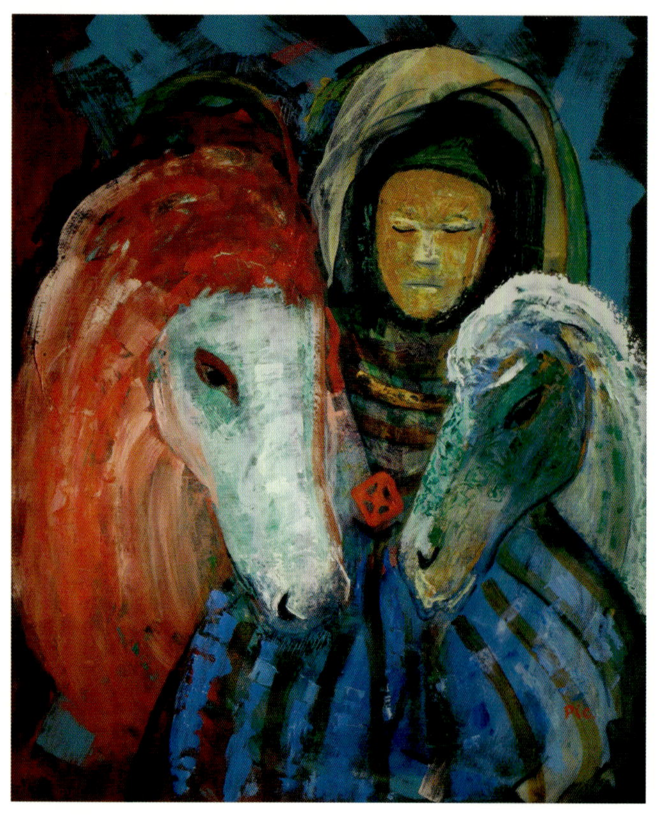

CHARLES S HIGGINS
(1893–1980)

56
Bedouin and Horses
Oil on board, 112.7 × 95 cm

Leicester Museums & Galleries:
Gift of Mrs Anne Kessler, 1983

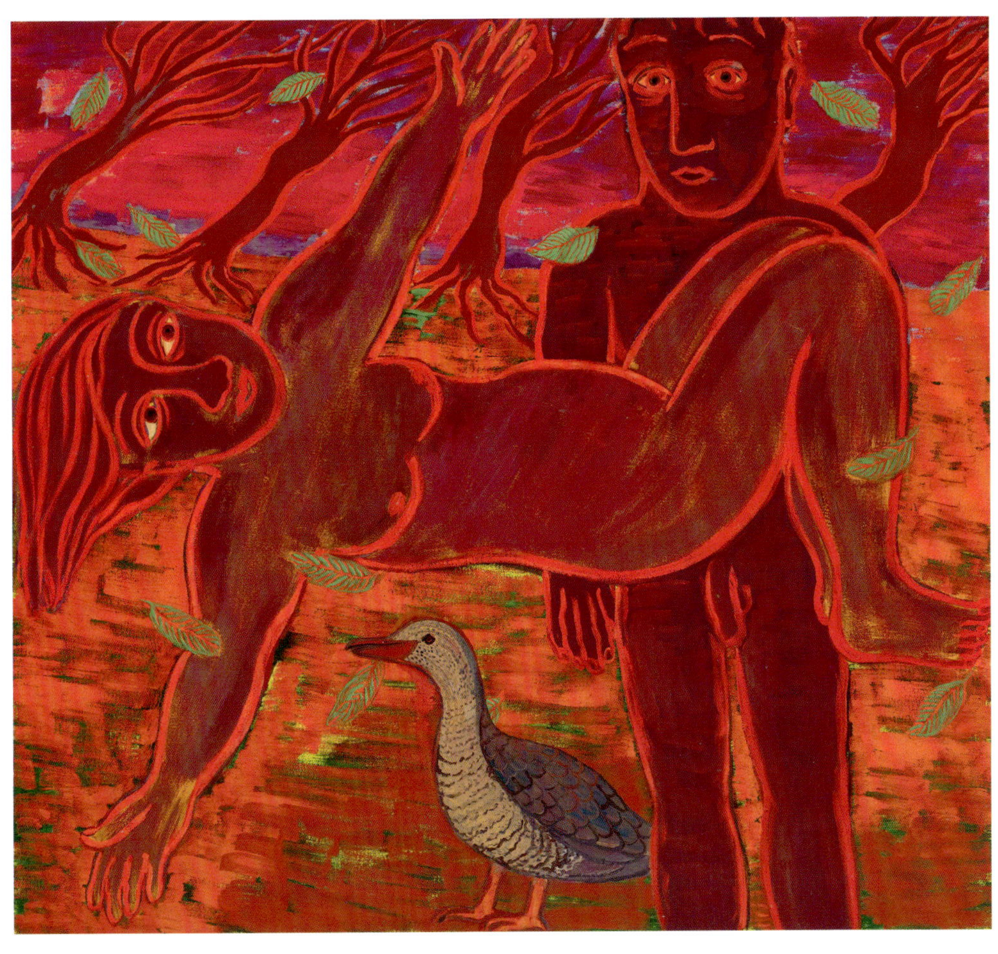

57
Floating Woman 1990
Oil on canvas, 152.5 × 165 cm

Eileen Cooper Family Collection

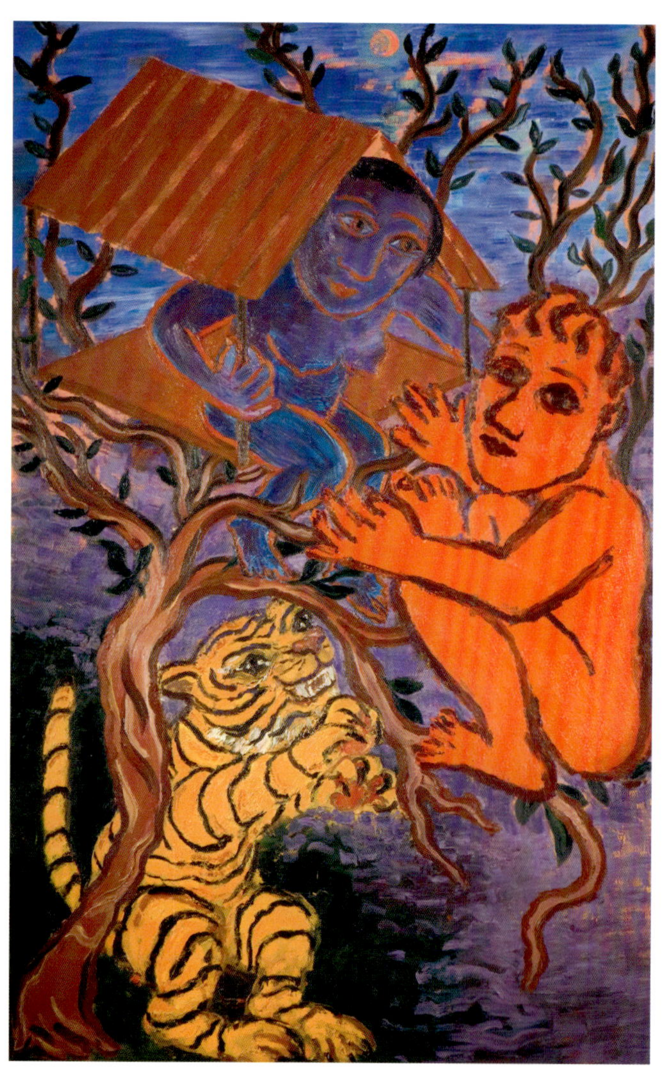

58
Tiger Tiger 1990
Oil on canvas, 168.5 × 126.5 cm

Wolverhampton Art Gallery

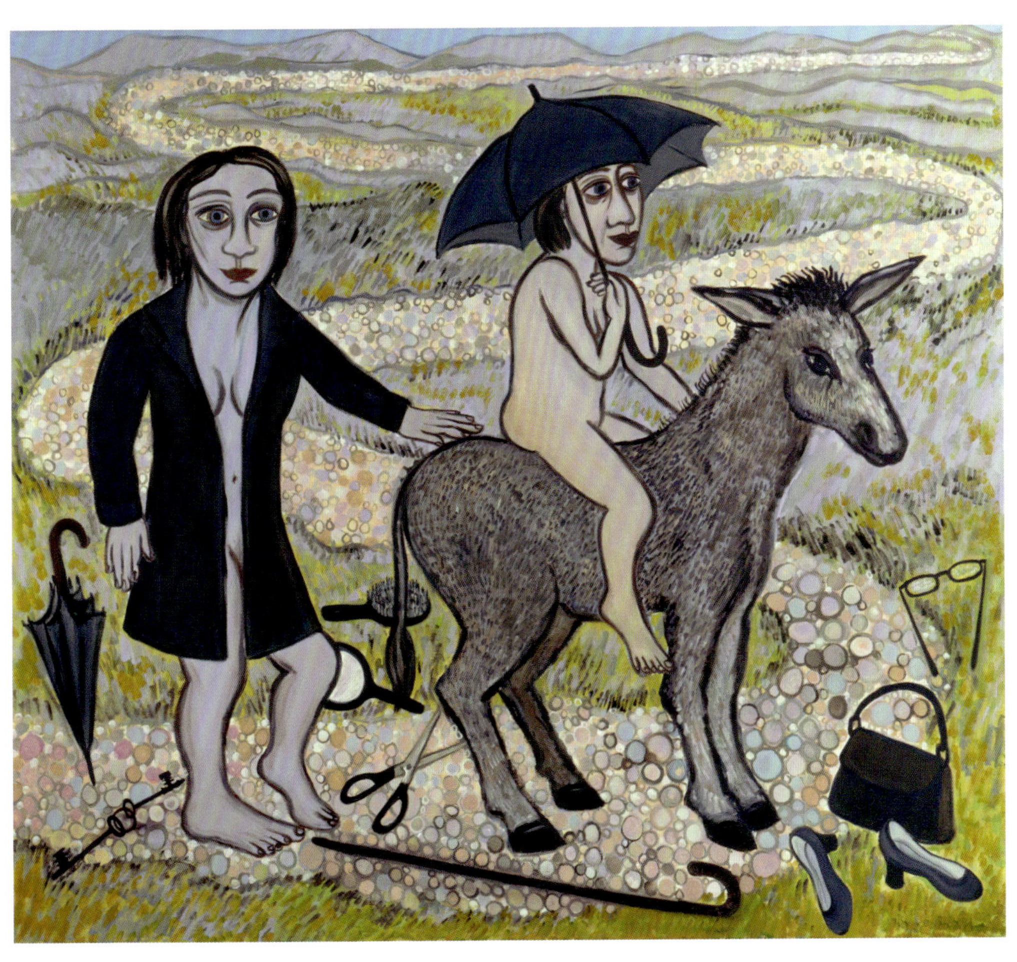

59
All Roads Lead... 2003
Oil on canvas, 137 × 153 cm

Private Collection

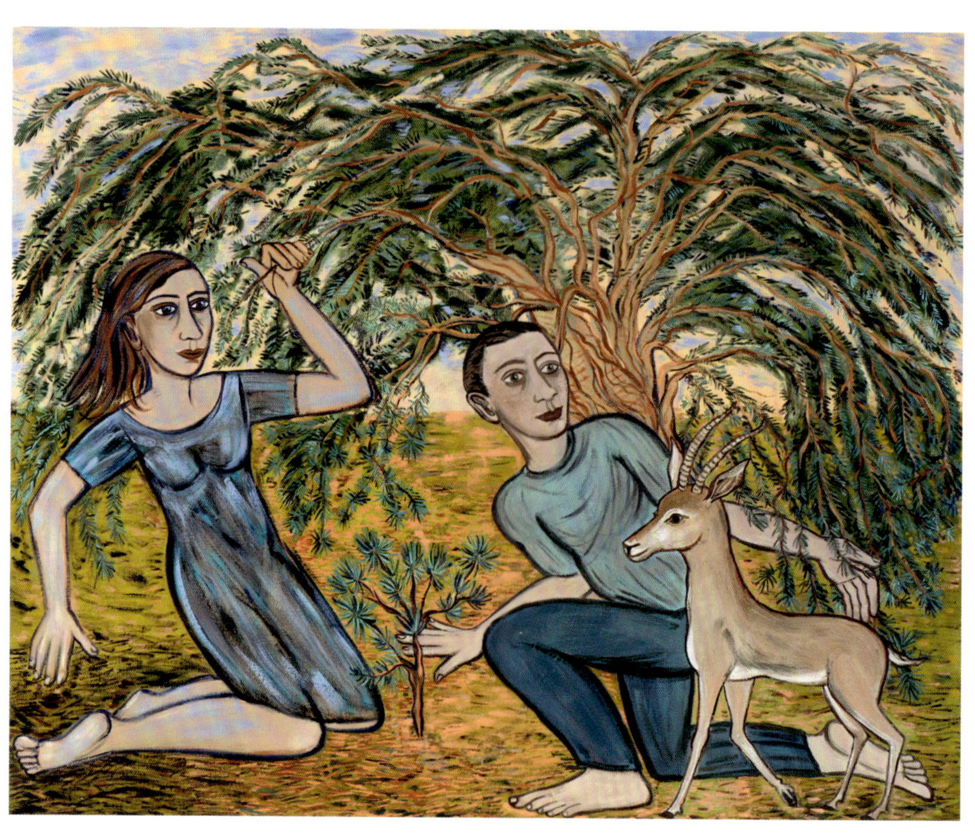

60
Evergreen 2018
Oil on canvas, 137 × 168 cm

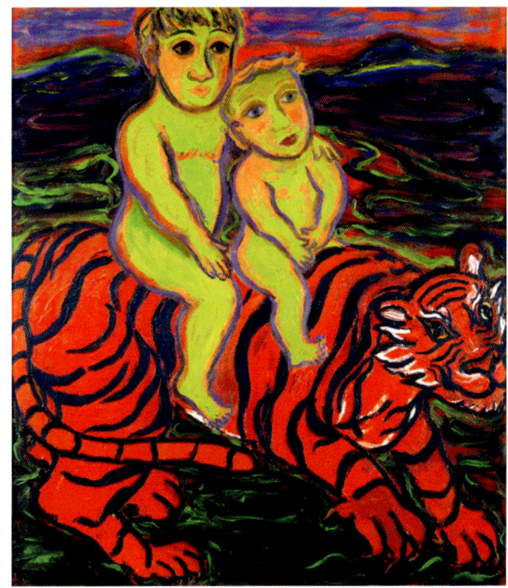

ii

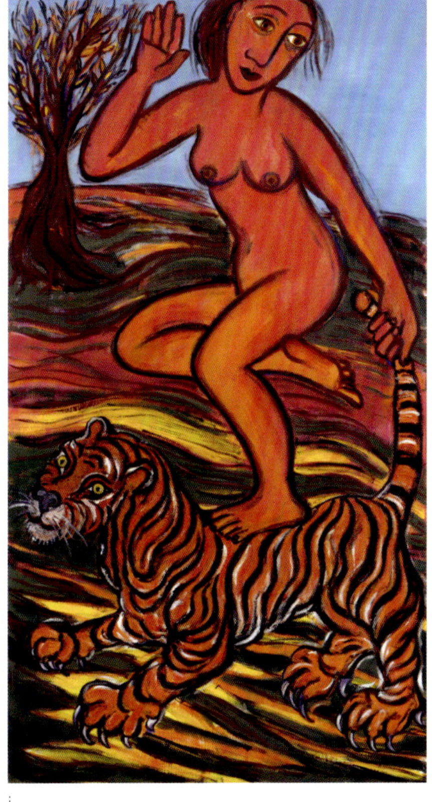

i

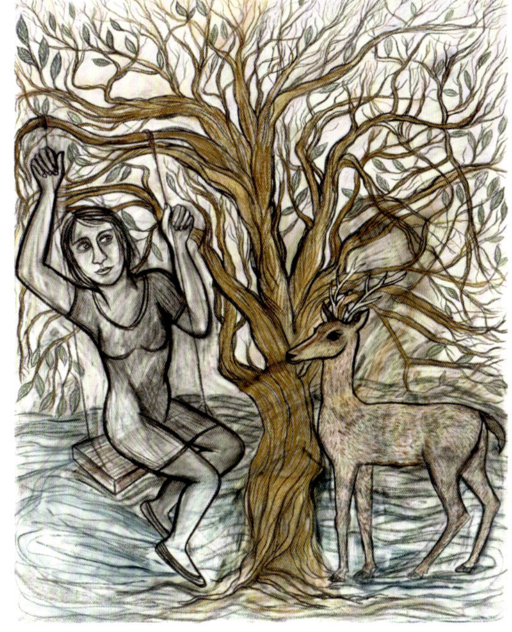

iii

i *Tail of the Tiger*, 2002, oil on canvas, 168 × 91 cm
ii *Boys and Tiger*, 1989–91, oil on canvas, 137 × 122 cm (Private Collection)
iii *The Great Unknown*, 2014, charcoal and pastel on paper, 137 × 122 cm (Private Collection)

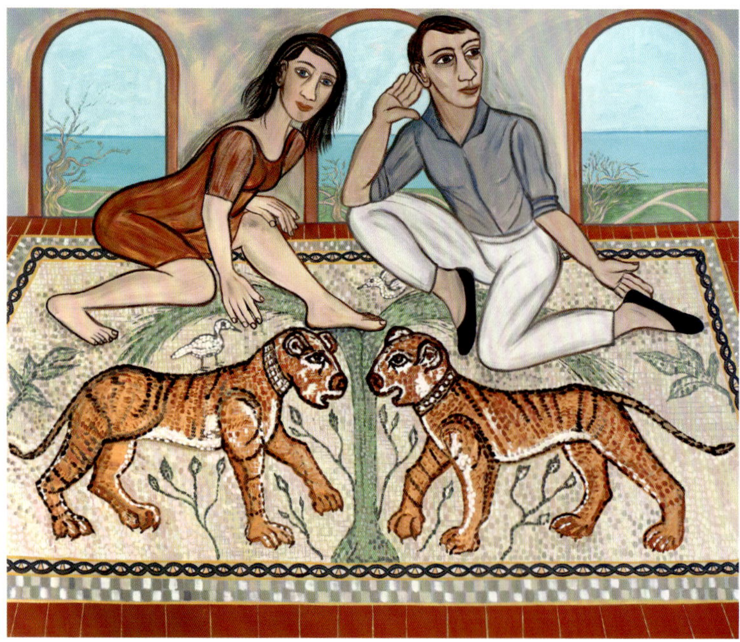

iv

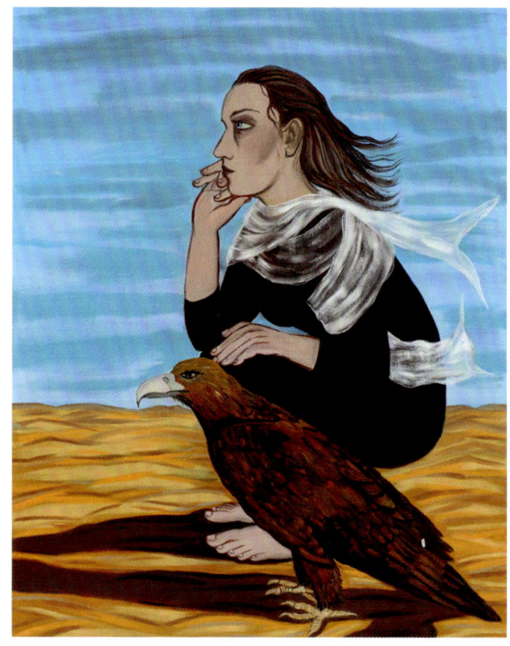

v

iv *Tiger Tiger*, 2018, oil on canvas, 153 × 183 cm (Private Collection)
v *Sixth Sense*, 2012, oil on canvas, 153 × 122 cm
vi *Chariot*, 2003, charcoal and pastel on paper, 122 × 153 cm (Private Collection)
vii *The Wanderers*, 2020, oil on canvas, 107 × 76 cm (Private Collection)
viii *Desire*, 2008, oil on canvas, 122 × 91 cm (Private Collection)

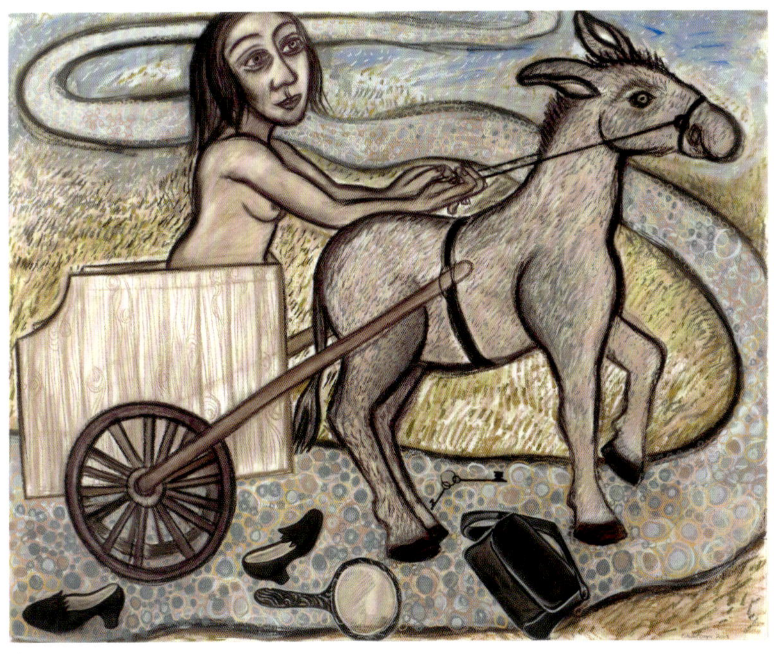

vi

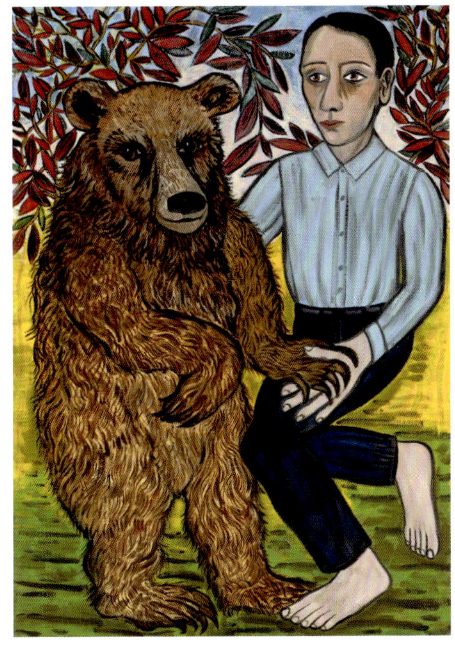

vii

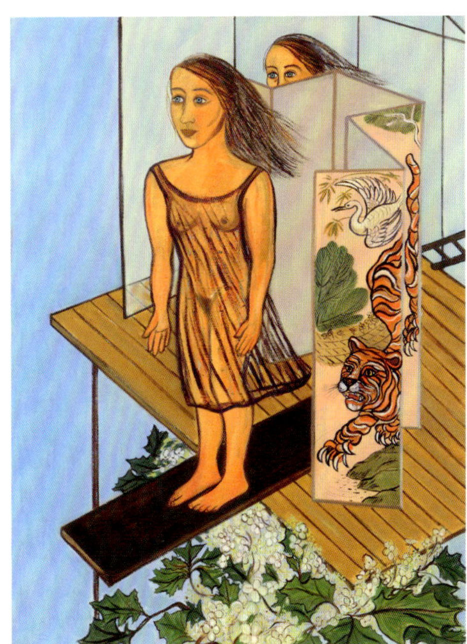

viii

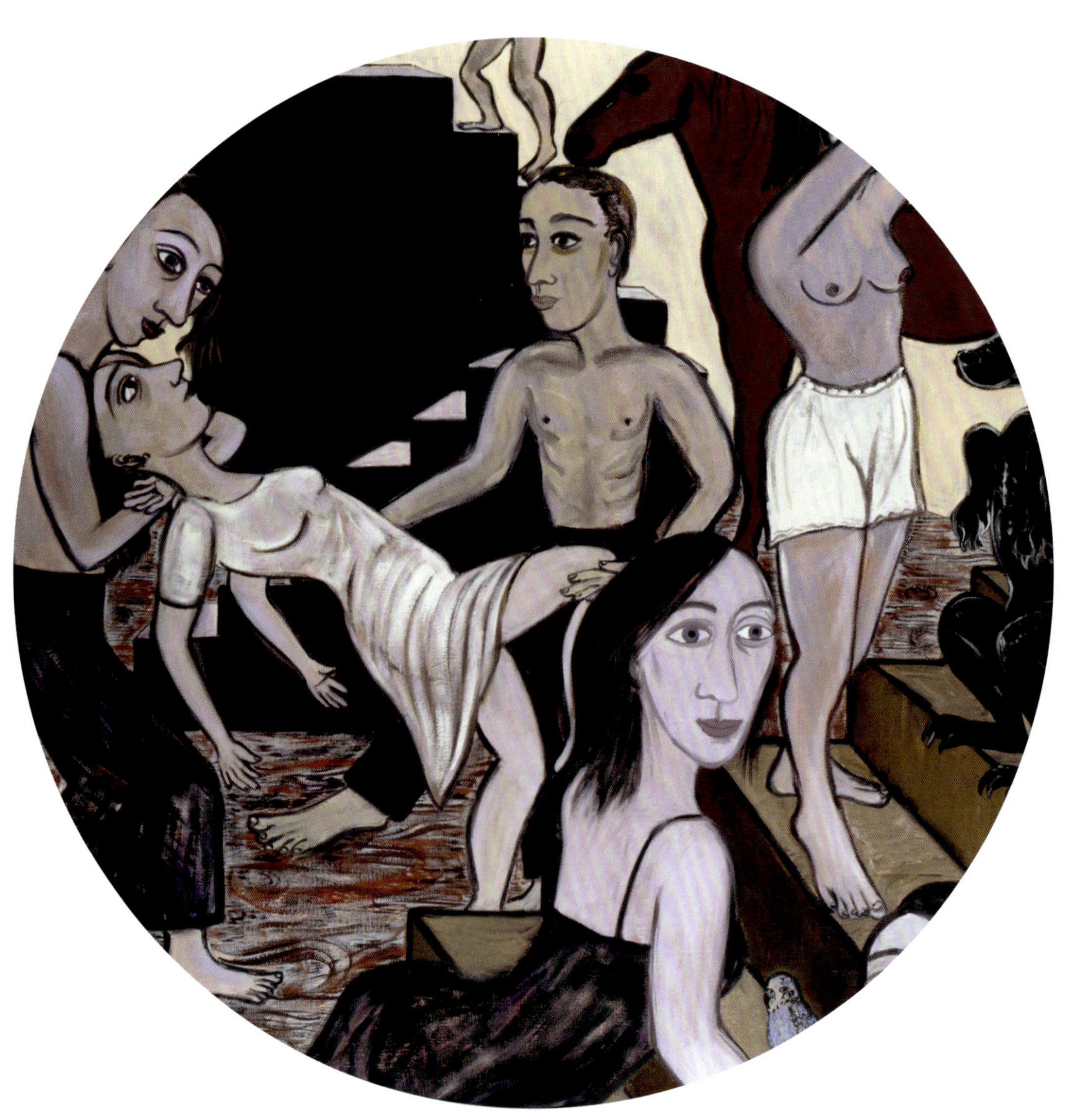

Detail: *Rehearsal* (p. 122)

9 DANCE

Dance has inspired artists through the ages, testing the physical capabilities of the human body, with its capacity for dynamism and expression. From country dances and ballet performances to can-can dancers, it has inspired artists from Henri Matisse and Edgar Degas to Paula Rego, Sonia Boyce and Lubaina Himid.

Dance and art have a long history of creative association. In the early 20th century Diaghilev revolutionised both worlds with his Ballets Russes. Picasso, Georges Braque, Natalia Goncharova and Sonia Delaunay were but a few artists to design his sets and costumes. The dancer Martha Graham and artist-designer Isamu Noguchi collaborated (1930s-80s), and in 1960s New York, choreographer Merce Cunningham developed performances with artists such as Robert Rauschenberg, Jasper Johns, Andy Warhol and Roy Lichtenstein. Today, many contemporary artists work with performance in which dance and choreography feature prominently.

Cooper's work is primarily pre-occupied with the physical body. It is often reduced in form, frequently simplified in its depiction, the idea of the universal body more important than likeness. However, there is a closer proximation to resemblance, and a more graphic representation that can be found in her work from around 2000. At the same time, movement in the works becomes more choreographed and the characters distinct, rather than seeming to merge into each other as they had previously. Figures act independently, or in partnership, supporting each other. This may reflect the shift in Cooper's life at this time, when focus moved away from the family, allowing a broader range of inspiration and concerns to begin to inform Cooper's work.

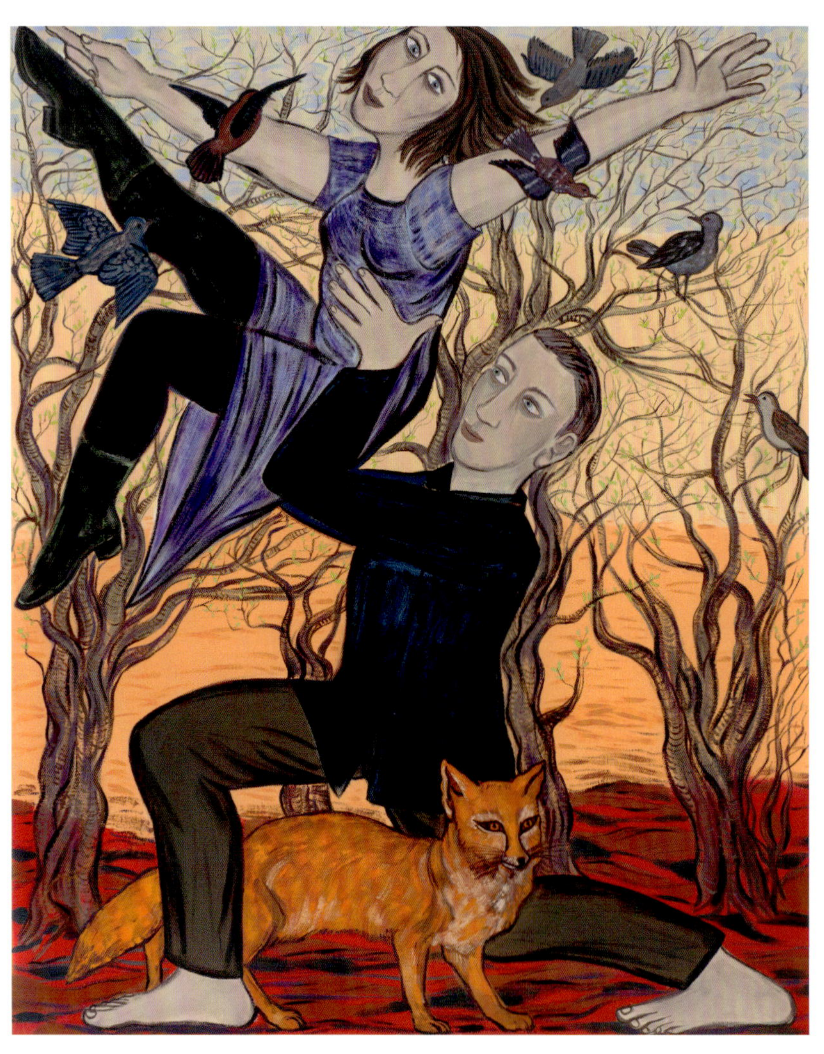

61
Spring Fever 2013
Oil on canvas, 168 × 137 cm

Private Collection

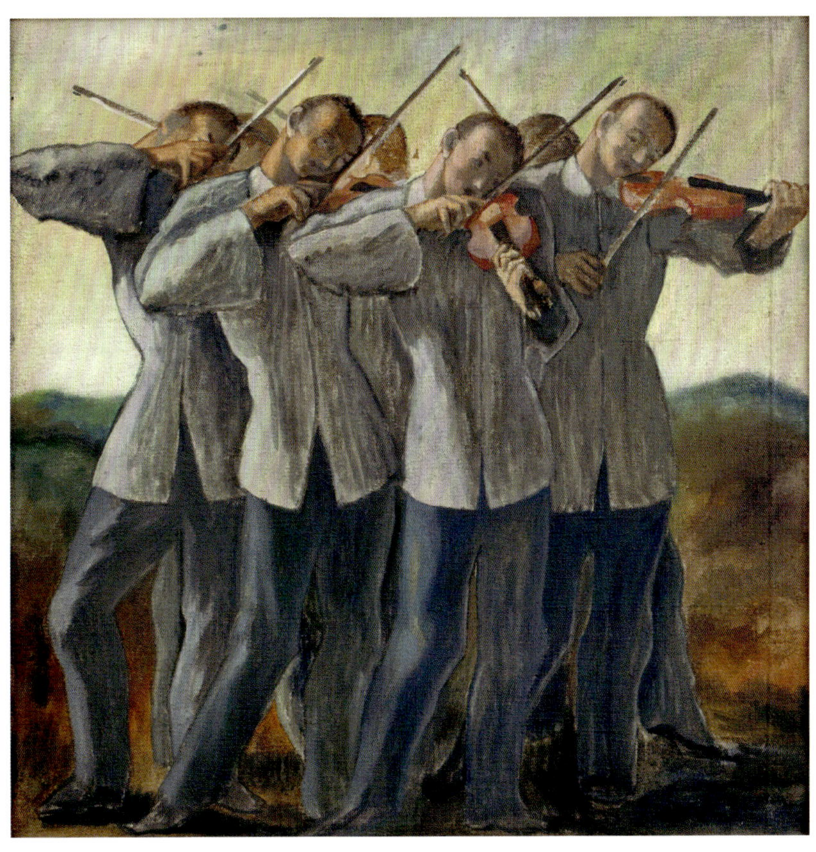

ARNOLD GERSTL
(1888–1956)

62
The Violinists
Oil on canvas, 109 × 109 cm

Leicester Museums & Galleries: Purchased from the artist with assistance from the MGC/V&A Purchase Grant Fund, 1989

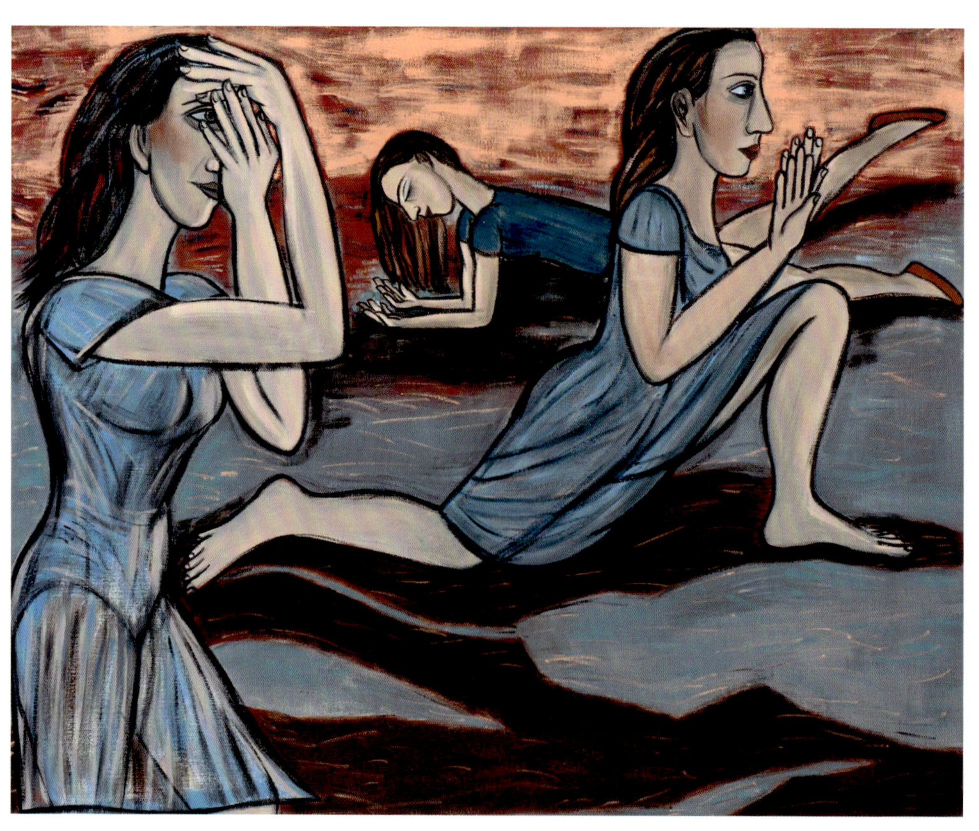

63
Silent Poetry 2017
Oil on canvas, 122 × 153 cm

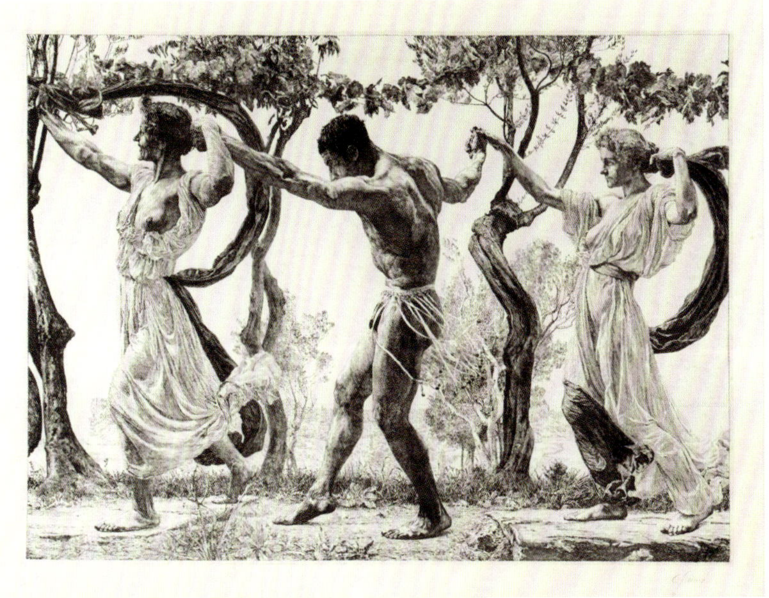

OTTO GREINER
(1869–1916)

64
The Dance 1896
Lithograph, 44 × 58 cm (55.2 × 67.8)

Leicester Museums & Galleries:
Purchased from Simon Reynolds, 1990

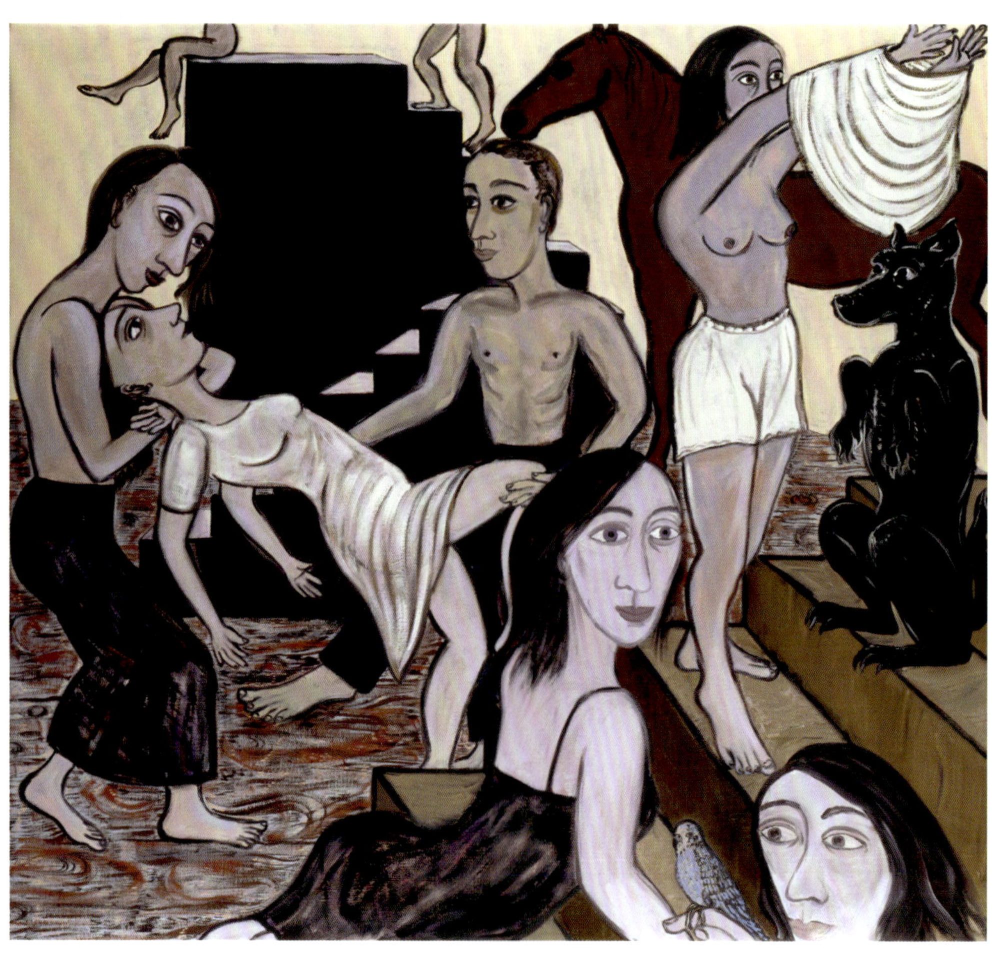

65
Rehearsal 2005
Oil on canvas, 152 × 168 cm

Private Collection

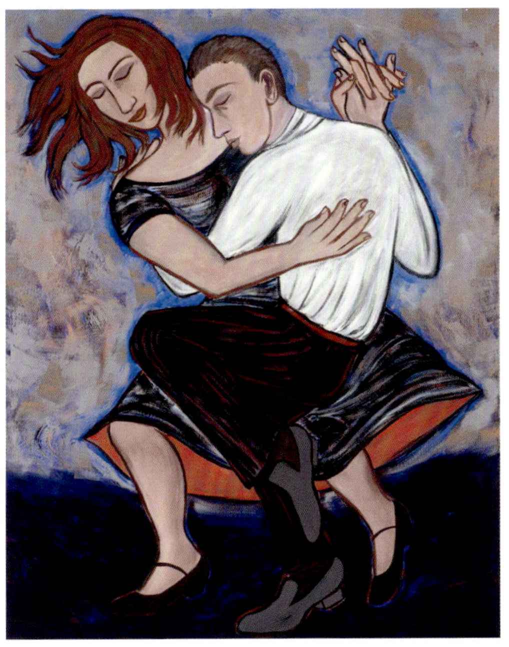
i

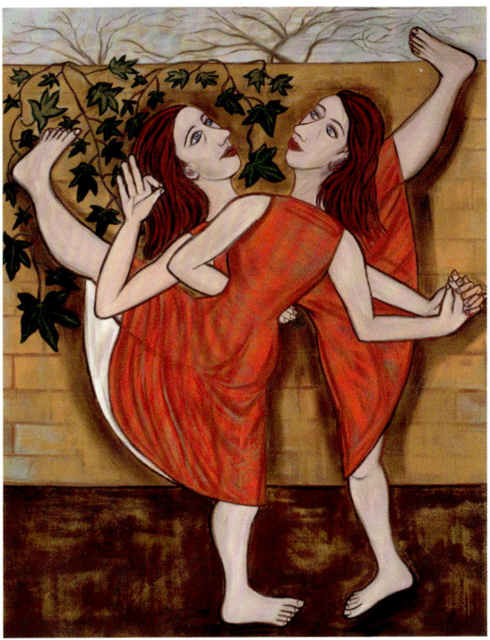
ii

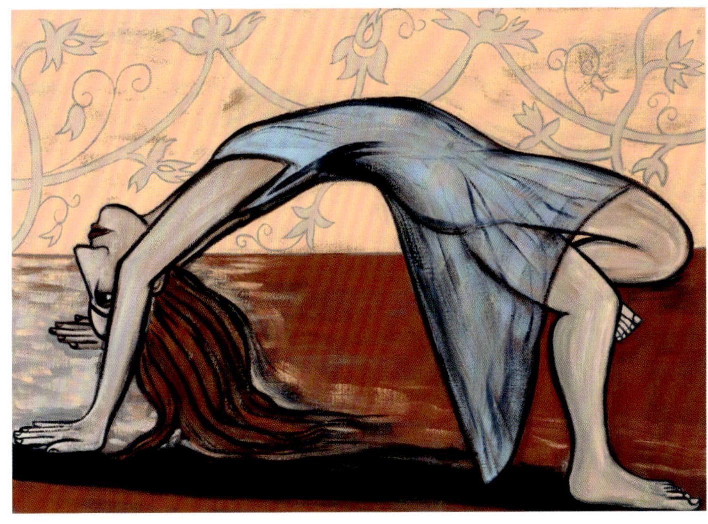
iii

i *Night Music*, 2015, oil on canvas, 153 × 122 cm
ii *Heavenly Day*, 2013–17, oil on canvas, 152 × 122 cm (Private Collection)
iii *Peace of Mind*, 2017, oil on canvas, 76 × 107 cm

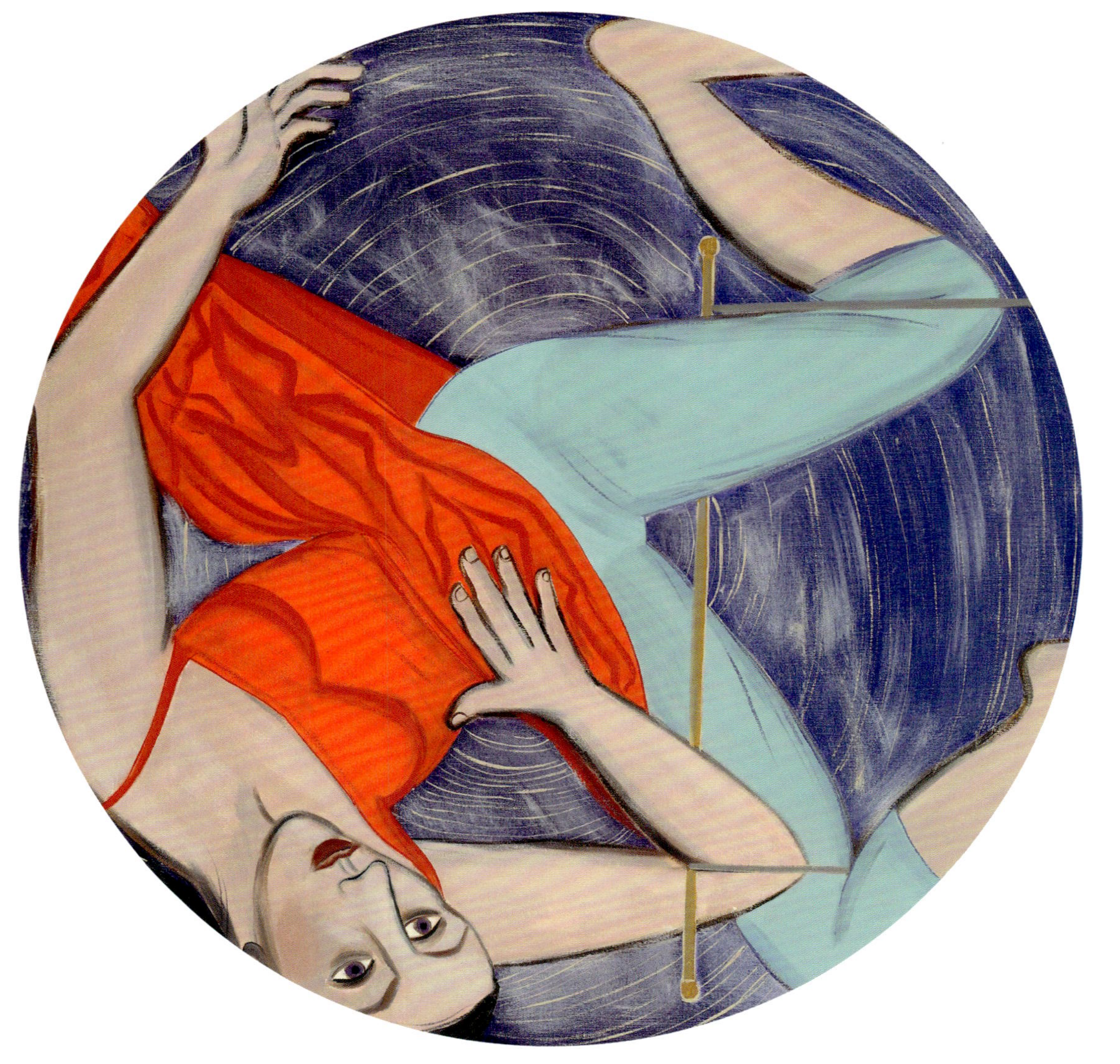

Detail: *Acrobat* (p. 128)

10 CIRCUS

The idea of circus is associated with freedom, a bohemian, itinerant lifestyle with performance and creativity at its heart. As the saying tells us, circus performers have run away from the traditional, hum-drum way of life embracing instead excitement, travel and the 'greatest show on earth'. Traditionally it was a visual spectacle, a place of colour, lights, drama and risk. It is no surprise therefore that it has inspired artists, who also associate themselves with the non-conformist, the unusual, the outsider looking in.

The circus ring is much like the artist's canvas, a space where the action takes place, the eye mesmerised and controlled by the activity that is happening within, shaped by the ringmaster, or in this case the artist.

As a child, Cooper remembers popular TV family entertainment featuring acrobatics, and the excitement of visits to Blackpool Tower Circus. In 1982 she visited Moscow on an art school trip where she took photographs of the Moscow State Circus. More recently, in 2020, Cooper engaged directly with the theme when commissioned to provide the illustrations for a new edition of Angela Carter's novel 'Nights at the Circus' for The Folio Society. Overall, the prevalence of balancing acrobats in Cooper's work may be an instinctive way in which she communicates danger, the struggles of life, the need to bend to demands, to rise above (on a trapeze), or simply to float away. Ultimately however it is a joyful and colourful subject that plays well to Cooper's intentions that her paintings engage and entertain with the stories contained within.

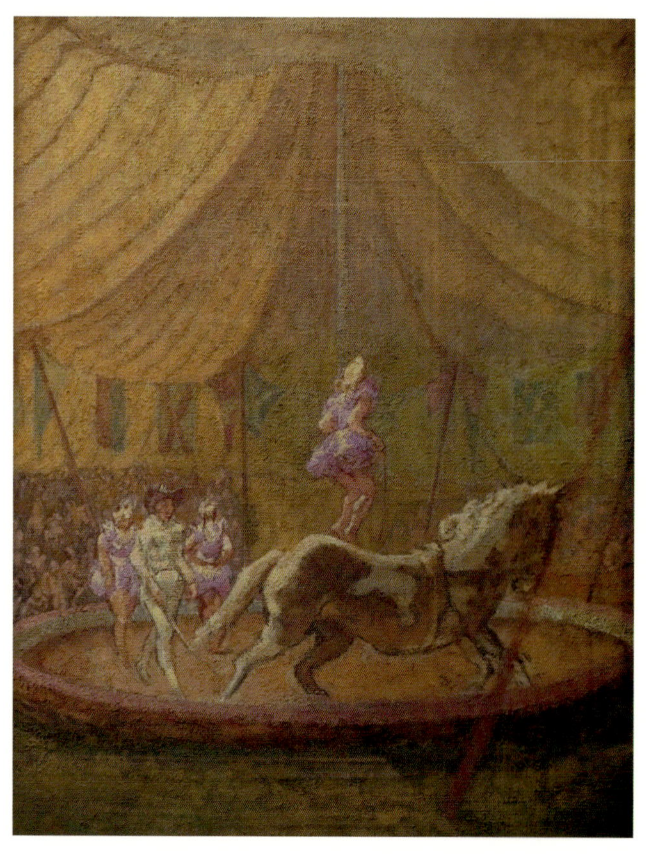

THÉRÈSE LESSORE
(1884–1945)

66
Circus at Bath
Oil on canvas, 88 × 68 cm

Leicester Museums & Galleries:
Gift of the Sickert Trust, 1947

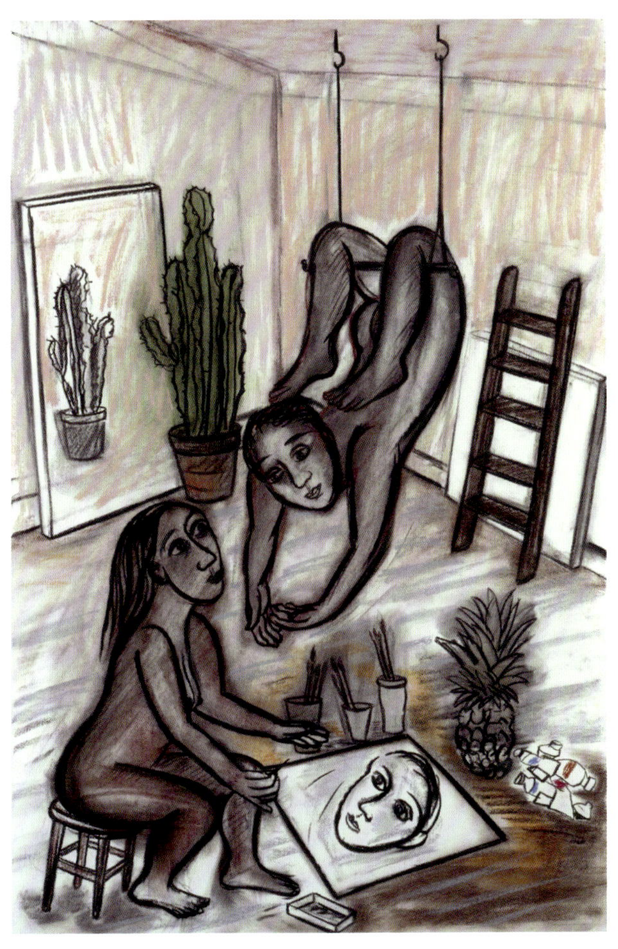

67
Boy on a Trapeze 2002
Charcoal and pastel on paper, 112 × 76 cm

Collection of Elizabeth and Rory Brooks

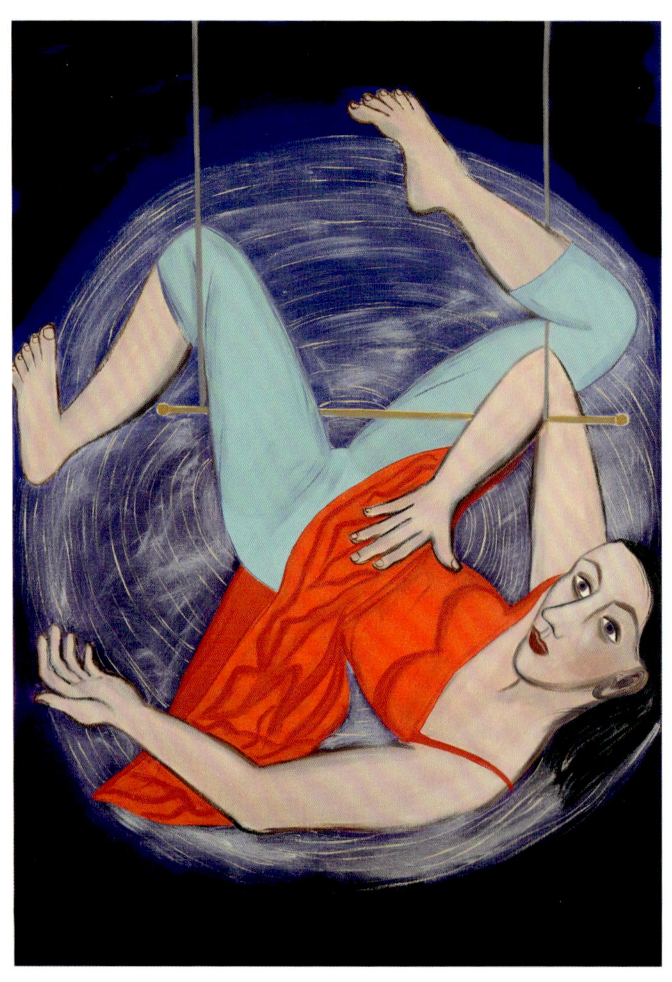

68
Acrobat 2011
Oil on canvas, 137 × 106.5 cm

Private Collection

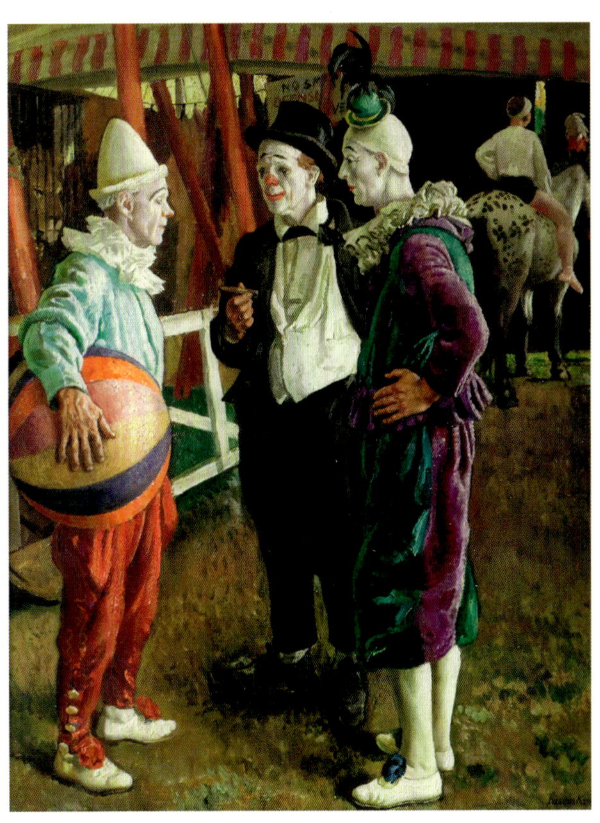

LAURA KNIGHT
(1877–1970)

69
The Three Clowns 1930
Oil on canvas, 77 × 63.5 cm

Leicester Museums & Galleries:
Purchased from the artist, 1934

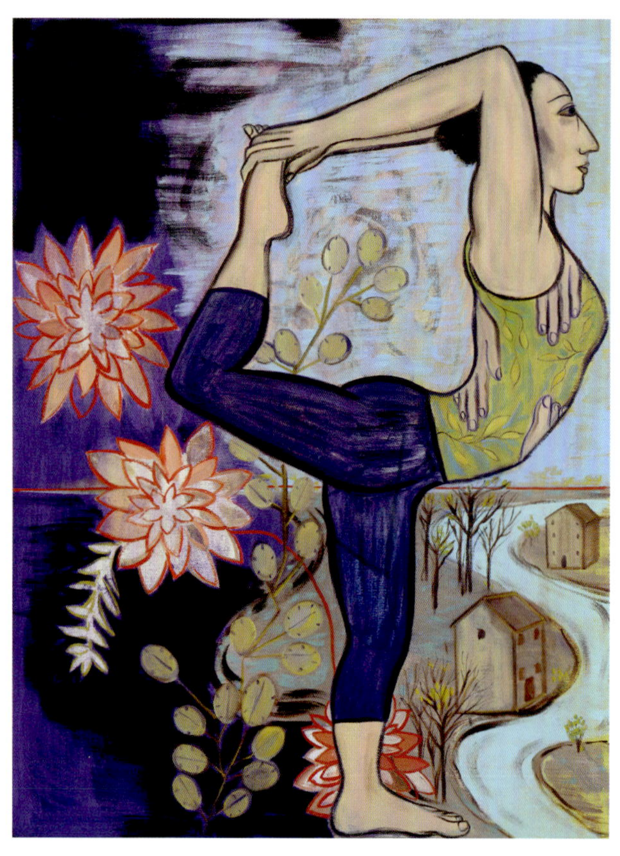

70
Freethinking 2012
Oil on canvas, 122 × 92 cm

Collection of Jeff Boardman

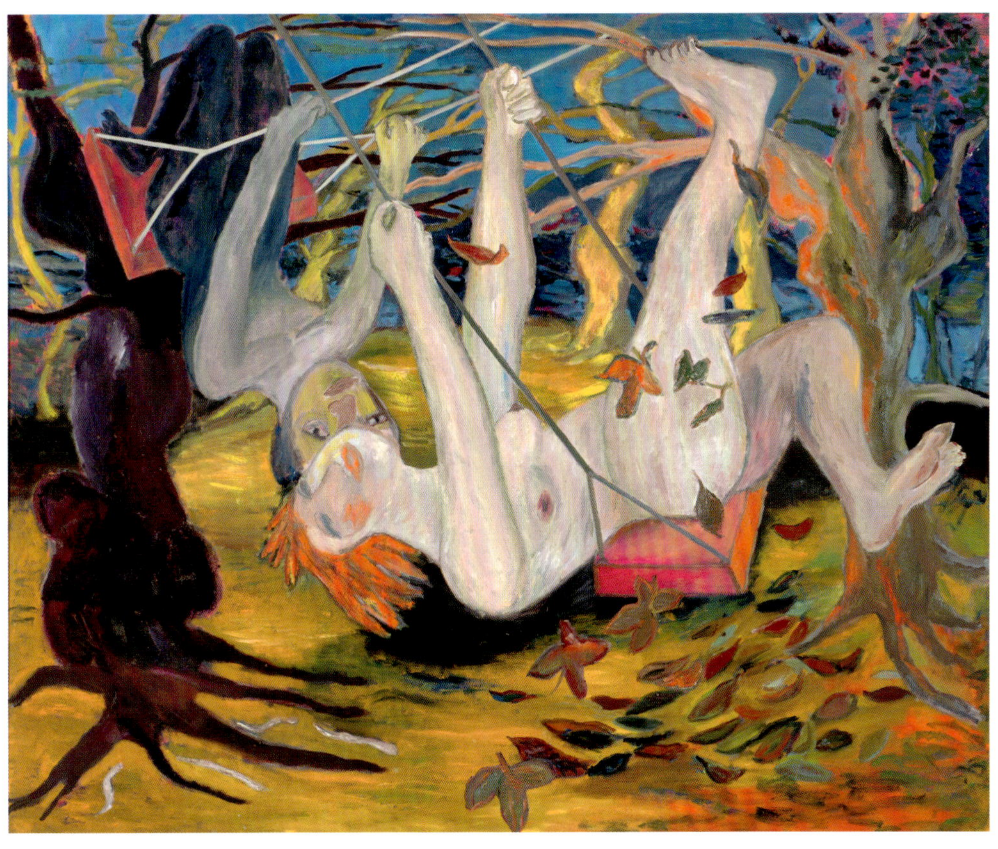

71
The Swing 1982
Oil on canvas, 126 × 156 cm

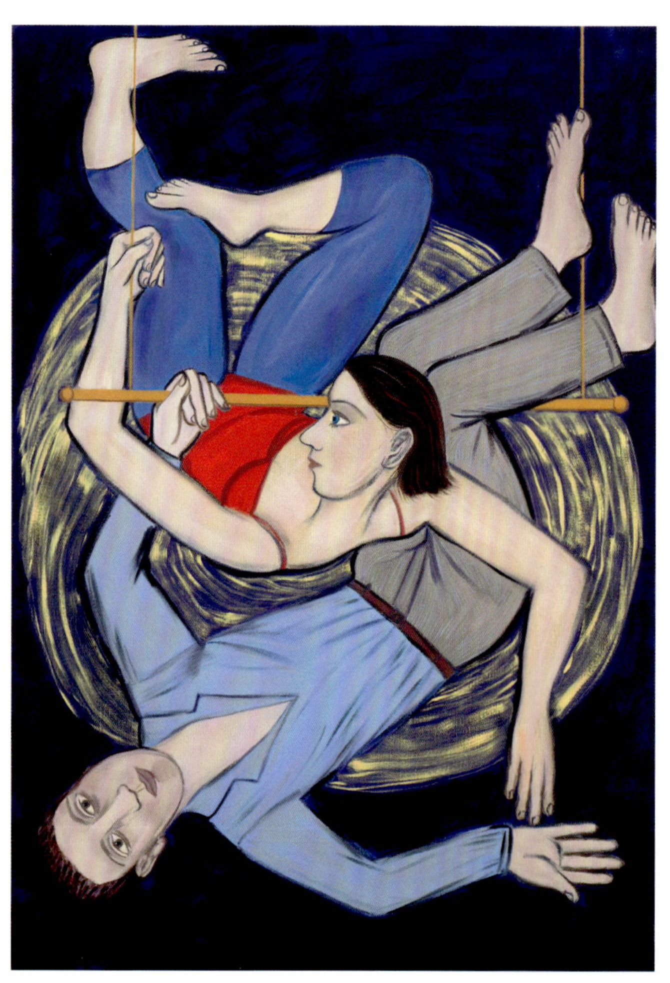

72
Trapeze 2012
Oil on canvas, 137 × 107 cm

Private Collection

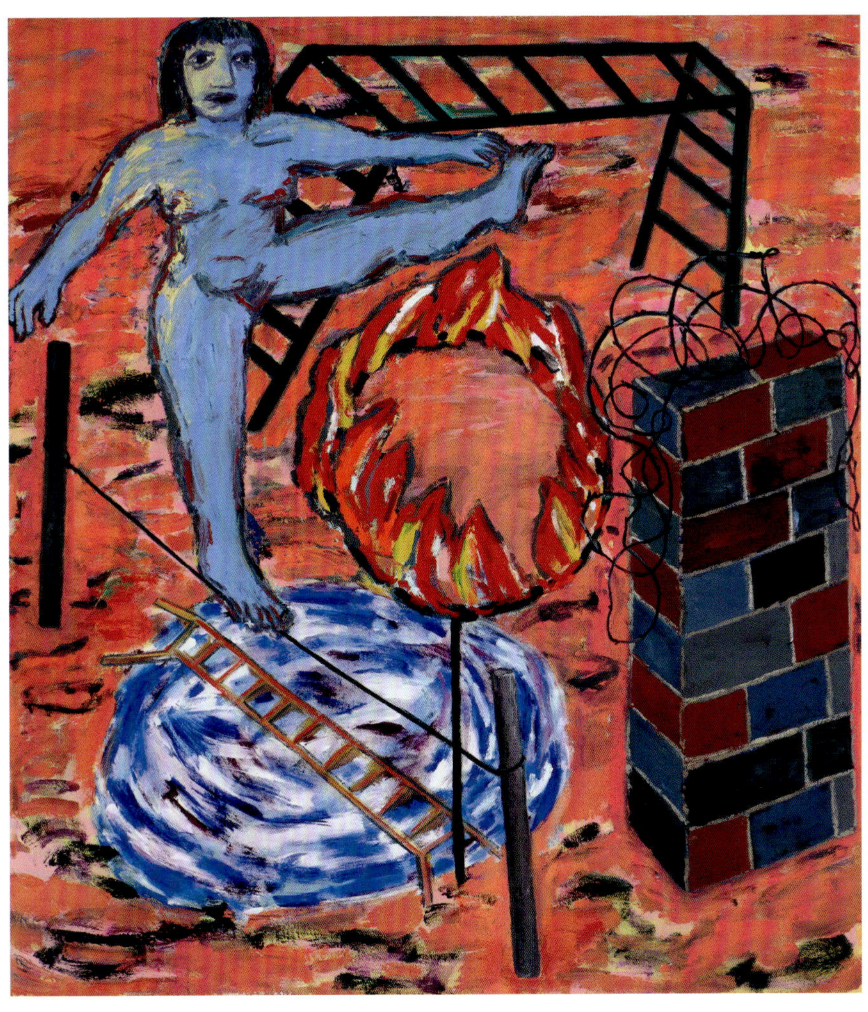

73
The Obstacle Course 1983
Oil on canvas, 155 × 140 cm

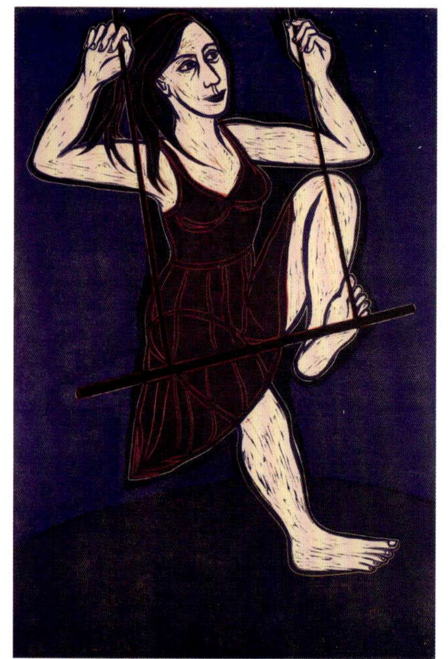

i

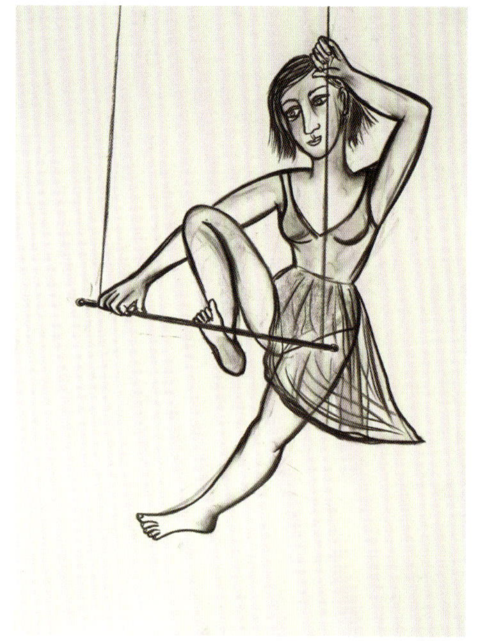

ii

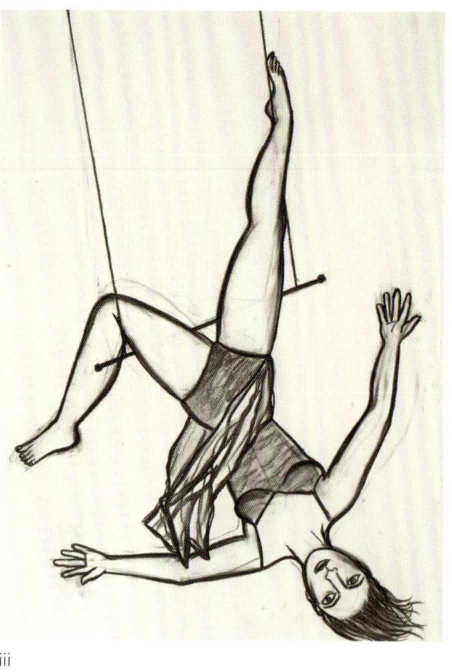

iii

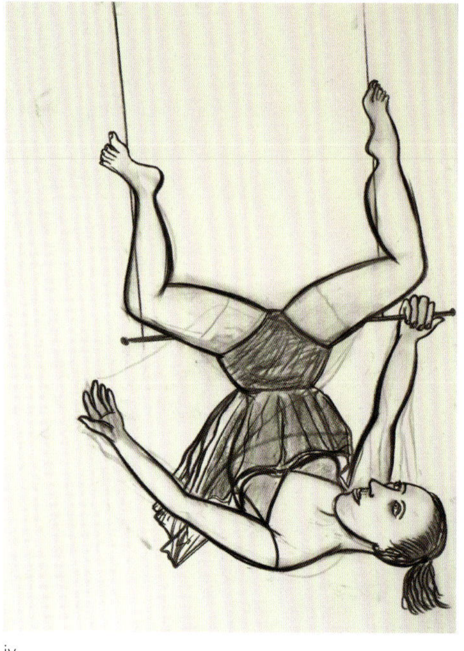

iv

i *Ariel*, 2016, woodcut, 96.5 × 66.5 cm
ii *Trapeze I*, 2012, charcoal on paper, 76 × 56 cm (Private Collection)
iii *Trapeze II*, 2012, charcoal on paper, 76 × 56 cm (Private Collection)
iv *Trapeze III*, 2012, charcoal on paper, 76 × 56 cm

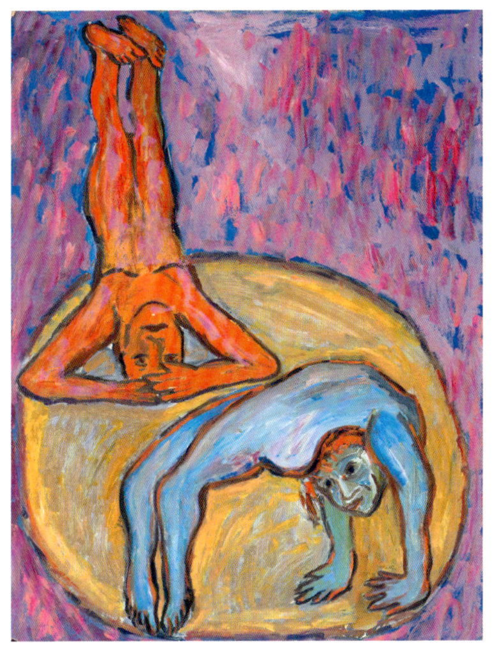

v

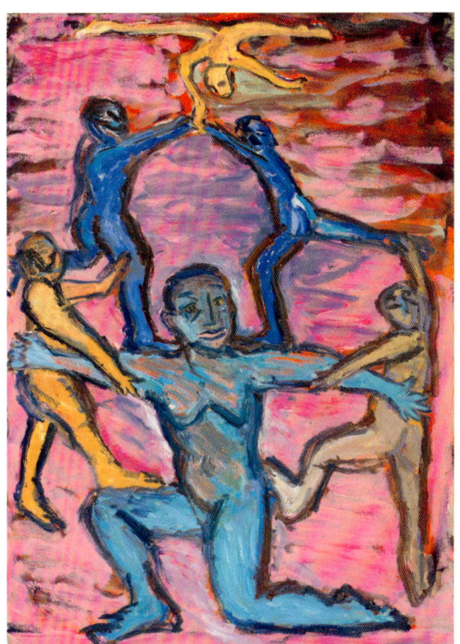

vi

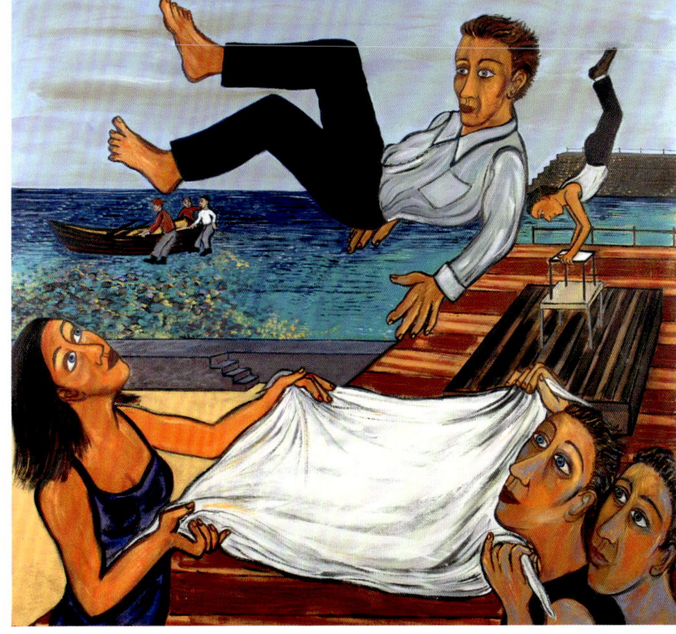

vii

v *Circus*, 1982, oil on card, 104 × 80 cm
vi *Tower of Strength*, 1982, oil on card, 104 × 80 cm
vii *Hero*, 2006, oil on canvas, 153 × 168 cm

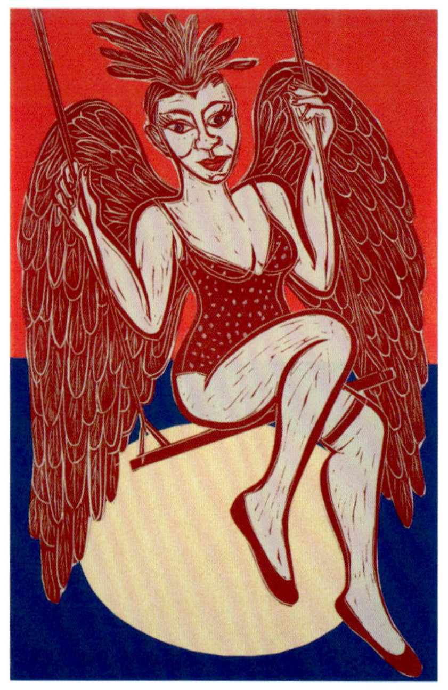

viii

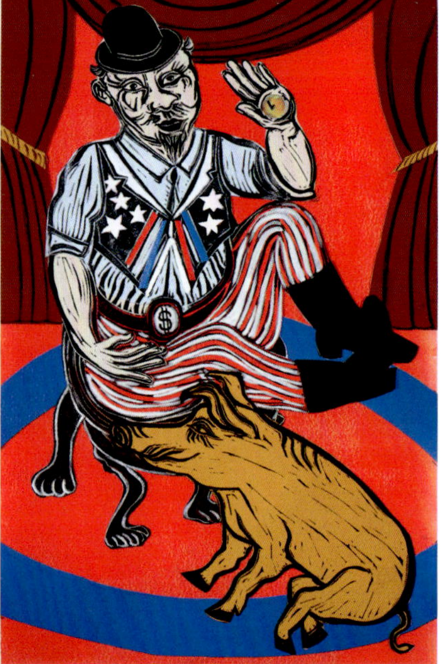

ix

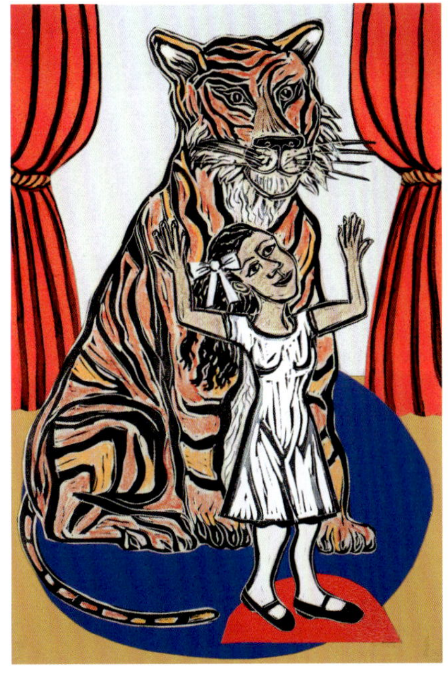

x

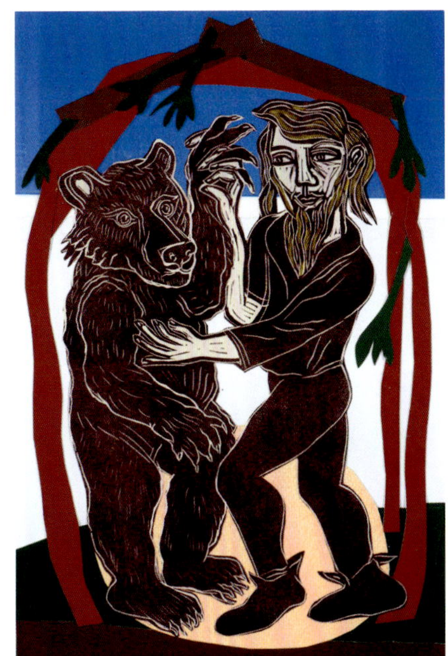

xi

From Angela Carter 'Nights at the Circus' series:
viii *Arieliste*
ix *The Ring Master*
x *Tiger and Princess*
xi *Dancing Bear*
All 2019, collage with monoprint, screenprint, pastel, ink and watercolour, 38 × 25.5 cm (Private Collection)

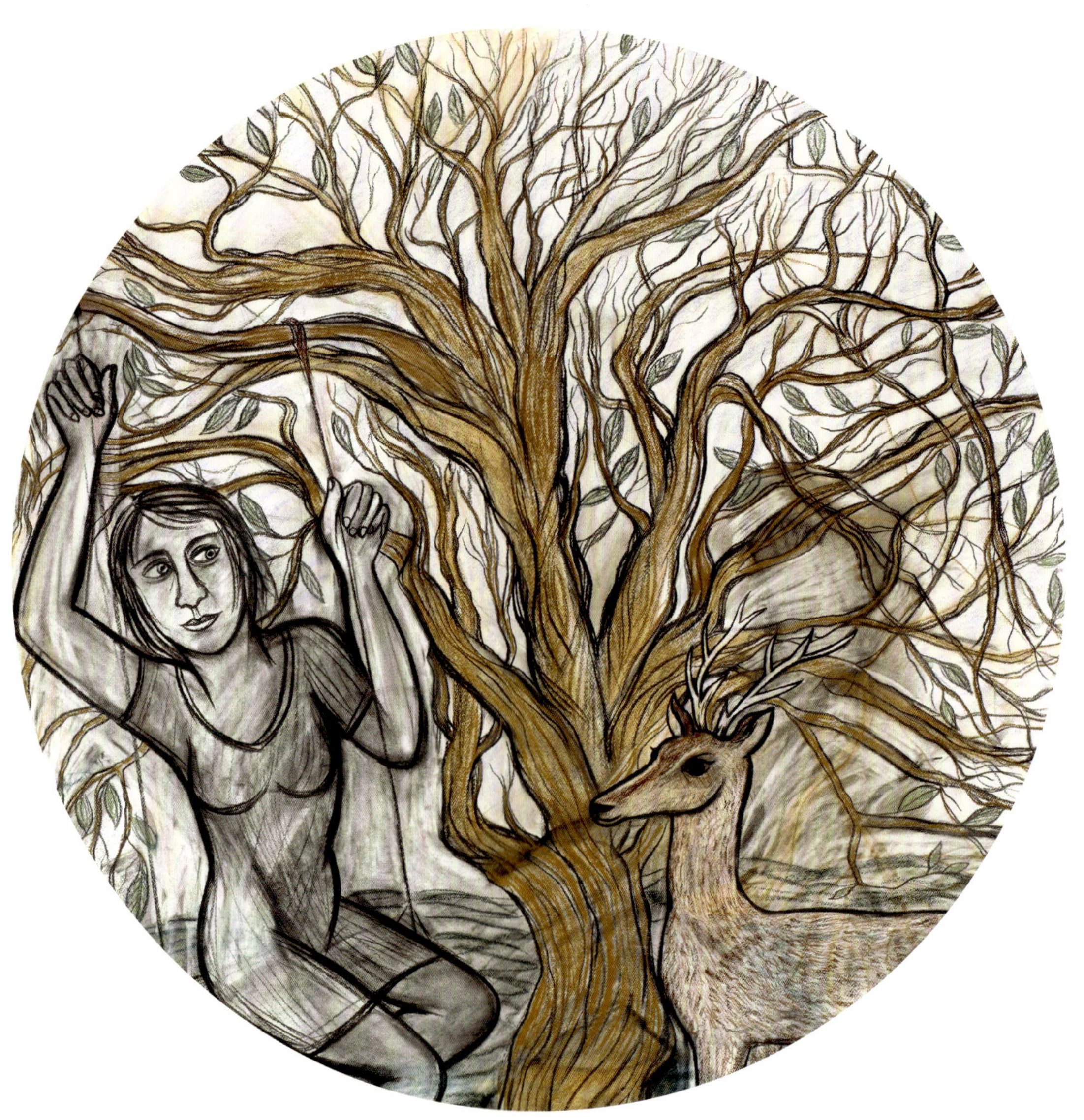

Detail: *The Great Unknown* (p. 113)

KATHLEEN SORIANO is an independent curator, strategic consultant and broadcaster. Chair of the Liverpool Biennial, a Trustee of Art UK, on the Visual Arts Committee of St Paul's Cathedral and Advisory Council of 2 Temple Place, she is also a specialist advisor to the National Trust. With over 35 years' experience in the art world she has been responsible for contemporary and historical exhibitions, collections and public programmes at the National Portrait Gallery, London and the Royal Academy of Arts, where she was Artistic Director (2009–14), as well as at Compton Verney Art Gallery, where she was previously Director. She has lectured and written extensively on art and her book *Madam and Eve* on women artists, co-authored with Liz Rideal, was published in April 2018. Her broadcast activities include the 'Portrait Artist of the Year' and the 'Landscape Artist of the Year' series for Sky Arts.

LINSEY YOUNG has held the position of Curator of British Contemporary Art at Tate Britain since 2016. In this role she has delivered commissions with artists such as Pablo Bronstein, Rachel Whiteread and Anthea Hamilton and is lead curator of the Turner Prize when it is held at Tate Britain. In 2019 she commissioned and curated Charlotte Prodger's presentation at the Venice Biennale and is currently working on 'Women in Revolt!' a major exhibition and publication project at Tate exploring art and the women's movement in the United Kingdom between 1970 and 1990.

EILEEN COOPER OBE RA

1953 Born Glossop, Derbyshire
1970–71 Ashton-under-Lyne College of Further Education
1971–74 Goldsmiths College, London
1974–77 Royal College of Art, London, MA Painting
1977–2000 Visiting lecturer at art schools throughout the UK, including Falmouth School of Art, Leicester College of Art and Design, St Martin's School of Art, Camberwell School of Arts and Crafts and City and Guilds of London Art School
1994–2006 Part time Lecturer in Printmaking at Royal College of Art
2005–2010 Head of Printmaking, Royal Academy Schools
2011–17 Keeper of the Royal Academy of Arts

Selected solo exhibitions

2022 *Parallel Lines: Eileen Cooper and Leicester's Art Collection*, Leicester Museum
Somewhere or Other, Huxley-Parlour Gallery, London
2021 *Nights at the Circus*, Sims Reed Gallery, London
2019 *Personal Space: New Paintings*, Huxley-Parlour Gallery, London
Short Stories, Sims Reed Gallery, London
2018 *Forest*, Rabley Gallery, Marlborough, Wiltshire
Under the Same Moon, Letitia Gallery, Beirut, Lebanon
2017 *Till the Morning Comes*, The Fine Art Society, London
Eileen Cooper: A Woman's Skin, Wolfson College, Cambridge
2016 *Love-in-Idleness*, Rook and Raven Gallery, London
Between the Lines, Galerie MIRO, Prague, Czech Republic
2015 *Hide and Seek, Drawing 1977–2014*, Royal Academy of Arts, touring to Swindon Museum and Art Gallery and The Mercer Art Gallery, Harrogate
Garden, Rabley Drawing Centre, Wiltshire
2013 *Edge to Edge*, Art First, London
2010 *Collages*, Royal Academy of Arts, London
2008 *Taking Stock: The Printmaking of Eileen Cooper RA*, Clifford Chance, London and The Cornerstone Gallery, Liverpool Hope University
2004 *Subject Matter – Paintings Drawings & Prints*, Glasgow Print Studio
2003 *Eileen Cooper at 50, A Celebration*, Art First, London and New York
2002 *Passions: New Work on Paper*, Art First, London and New York
2000 *Raw Material: Eileen Cooper at Dulwich Picture Gallery*, London
1999 *Second Skin: Eileen Cooper in the 80s and 90s*, touring: Wolverhampton, Nottingham and Eastbourne
1998 *Graphic Work*, Bridport Arts Centre, Dorset
1996–97 *New Graphic Works*, touring: Darlington, Harrogate and Scarborough
1994 *Eileen Cooper at Sadlers Wells Theatre*, London
1993–94 *Lifelines*, touring: Lancaster, Exeter, Newcastle, Brighton, Sheffield and Warwick
1990 *Paintings, Drawings and Prints*, Benjamin Rhodes Gallery, London
1988 Benjamin Rhodes Gallery, London
1986 Castlefield Gallery, Manchester
1983 Blond Fine Art, London
1982 Blond Fine Art, London
1979 AIR Gallery, London

Selected group exhibitions

2022 *Act 1: Body en Thrall with the Rugby Collection*, Rugby Art Gallery and Museum
An Ode to Orlando, Pi Artworks, 55 Eastcastle St, London

2021 *Hockney to Himid : 60 Years of British Printmaking*, Pallant House Gallery, Chichester

2020 *Graphic Impact: Our Lives in Print*, Glasgow Print Studio, Glasgow

2019 *Women Artists in Conversation with Partou Zia*, Falmouth Art Gallery, Cornwall

2018 *Sawdust and Sequins: The Art of the Circus*, Royal West of England Academy

2017 *Women Artists: a Conversation*, The Fine Art Society, London

2016 *Strange Worlds: The Vision of Angela Carter*, Royal West of England Academy, Bristol
Towards Night, Towner Art Gallery, Eastbourne

2014 *Jerwood Drawing Prize 1994–2014: Artist as Selector*, Jerwood Gallery, Hastings
Embrace, The Wilson, Cheltenham Art Gallery and Museum

2013–14 *RA Portfolio Diamond Jubilee Gift*, Queens Gallery, Buckingham Palace, London

2012–13 *Encounter, The Royal Academy in the Middle East*, Cultural Village Foundation-Katara, Doha, Qatar

2012 *Encounter, The Royal Academy in Asia*, Institute of Contemporary Arts, Singapore
The Mechanical Hand: 25 Years of Printmaking at Paupers Press, Kings Place Gallery, London

2007 *Leben Lieben*, RISE Gallery, Berlin

2006 *Drawing Breath – 10 Years of the Jerwood Annual*, Wimbledon College of Art, London and touring: UK and Sydney, Australia

2004 *The Jerwood Drawing Prize*, Jerwood Space, London
Tradition and Innovation, Scarborough Museum and Art Gallery

1999–2000
Hand To Hand (with Julian Stair), Shipley Art Gallery, Gateshead and Art First, London

1998 *The Contemporary Print Show Part I*, Barbican Centre, London

1997 *The Body Politik*, Wolverhampton Art Gallery

1996 *Spirit on the Staircase, 100 Years of Print Publishing*, Royal College of Art, Victoria & Albert Museum, London

1994–95 *An American Passion*, The Susan Kasen Summer & Robert D Summer Collection of Contemporary Painting, McLellan Galleries, Glasgow and Royal College of Art, London

1993 *Contemporary Art at the Courtauld*, Courtauld Institute, London

1992 *The New Patrons, Twentieth Century Art from Corporate Collections*, Christie's, London
Myth, Dream and Fable, Angel Row Gallery, Nottingham
Innocence and Experience, South Bank Centre, London and Manchester City Art Gallery, touring: Hull, Nottingham and Glasgow
20th Century Women's Art, New Hall, Cambridge

1991–92 *Look Here Upon This Picture and On This*, selected by Norbert Lynton, South Bank Centre, touring exhibition

1991 *The Outsider: British Figuration Now*, Palazzo Vecchio, Florence, Italy
Postmodern Prints, Victoria & Albert Museum, London

1989 *Picturing People*, British Council tour: Kuala Lumpur, Hong Kong and Singapore

1988 *The New British Painting*, Contemporary Arts Center, Cincinnati and touring (USA)

1987 *Conversations*, Arts Council touring exhibition

1986 *The Flower Show*, Stoke-on-Trent Museum
John Moores, Walker Art Gallery, Liverpool

1985–87 *International Biennial of Graphic Art*, Ljubljana, Yugoslavia

1985 *The Passion and The Power*, Gracie Mansion Gallery, New York
International Festival of Painting, Cagnes sur Mer, France
Proud and Prejudice, selected by William Feaver, Twining Gallery, New York

1984 *The Image as Catalyst*, Ashmolean Museum, Oxford

1982/83/87
Whitechapel Open, Whitechapel Art Gallery, London

1982 *Nuremberg Drawing Triennial* (Purchase Prize)

1980 Women's Images of Men, ICA, London

1977–2022
Royal Academy Summer Exhibition, Royal Academy of Arts, London

1974–76 *New Contemporaries Exhibition*, Camden Arts Centre, London

Awards and commissions

2022 Honorary Academician of the Royal West of England Academy
2021 Cover and illustrations for *Nights at the Circus* by Angela Carter, The Folio Society
2017 Coordinator, Royal Academy Summer Exhibition
2016 OBE for services to Art and Art Education
2016 Honorary Fellow, Murray Edwards College, Cambridge
2014 Honorary Doctor of Arts, Southampton Solent University
2010, 2013, 2019 Artist in residence, Alayrac, France
2011–17 Elected Keeper of the Royal Academy of Arts
2011 Honorary Fellow, Royal College of Art
2009 Curator and coordinator, Royal Academy Summer Exhibition
2009 Selector, *Originals*, Mall Galleries, London,
2008–09 Artist in residence, Lewisham College
2006 Fellow, Royal College of Art
2002 Honorary Member of the Royal Society of Painter-Printmakers
2001 Elected Royal Academician
1999 Arts & Humanities Research Board, Award for Ceramic work, Ceramics from a Fine Artist
1999 Cover and illustrations for *Meeting Midnight* by Carol Ann Duffy, Faber & Faber
1998–99 Artist in residence, Dulwich Picture Gallery, London
1986 Frontispiece for *Thrown Voices* by Carol Ann Duffy, published by Bernard Stone
1982 Staircase Project, ICA, London
1982 Purchase Prize, Nuremberg Drawing Triennial

Selected public collections

Arts Council Collection
Birmingham Museums and Art Gallery
Bristol Museum and Art Gallery
British Council
British Museum
Dallas Museum of Art
Imperial College, London
Kunsthalle, Nuremberg
Manchester Art Galleries
Mercer Art Gallery, Harrogate
MIMA, Middlesborough
National Portrait Gallery, London
Newport Art Gallery
Open University, Milton Keynes
Otter Gallery, University of Chichester
Pallant House, Chichester
The Potteries Museum and Art Gallery, Stoke-on-Trent
Royal Academy of Arts
Royal Collection
Southampton City Art Gallery
Swindon Art Gallery
Towner Art Gallery, Eastbourne
University of Warwick Art Collection
Victoria and Albert Museum, London
Walpole Library, Yale University, USA
Whitworth Art Gallery, Manchester
Wolverhampton Art Gallery
The Women's Art Collection, Murray Edwards College, Cambridge

---

Edited by Kathleen Soriano
Copy-editing and proofreading by Gill Crabbe
Design by Malcolm Southward
Colour origination and print by Gomer Press, Wales

Editorial Note
All dimensions are in centimetres
Dimensions for paintings and works on paper are unframed height × width
Dimensions for prints are first plate/block size, (second paper size)
All works by Eileen Cooper belong to the artist unless otherwise stated

Acknowledgements

With special thanks to
Eileen Cooper
Mark Holt
Giles Huxley-Parlour and the team at Huxley-Parlour Gallery
Julia Peintner
Kathleen Soriano
Malcolm Southward
Iliana Taliotis
Linsey Young
The staff at Leicester Museums, and especially:
Claire Cooper
Spencer Greasley
James Hickford
Harjeet Kaur
Mark Simmons
Heather Southern
Simon Watkins
All lenders to the exhibition

Exhibition supporters
William Brake Family Trust
Charles and Hen Irving
Martin McGowan, Blue Apron Transport Ltd
John Talbot

Photography credits

Photography of Eileen Cooper works by Justin Piperger and Todd-White.

All images of Leicester Museums & Galleries' works are courtesy of Leicester Museums & Galleries.

Every attempt has been made to trace copyright holders. We apologise for any inadvertent infringement and invite appropriate rights holders to contact us.

Fig: **1** (p. 28) © Paula Rego. Courtesy the Artist, Leicester Museums & Galleries, and Victoria Miro; **3** (p.30) © Peter Doig. All rights reserved, DACS 2022; **6** (p. 33) © The Estate of Francis Bacon. All rights reserved. DACS 2022; **7** (p. 34) © the copyright holder; **11** (p. 42) © DACS 2022; **13** (p. 44) © DACS 2022; **16** (p. 47) © DACS 2022; **17** (p.48) © the copyright holder; **24** (p. 58) © DACS 2022; **28** (p. 61) © the copyright holder; **31** (p. 64) © the Artist; **33** (p. 72), **36** (p. 75), **39** (p. 78), **43** (p. 81) © Succession Picasso/DACS, London 2022; **37** (p. 76) © the Artist; **44** (p. 84) © the copyright holder; **47** (p. 87) © the copyright holder; **48** (p. 92) © the copyright holder; **51** (p. 98) © the copyright holder; **53** (p. 100) © the copyright holder; **56** (p. 108) © the copyright holder; **62** (p. 119) © Arnold Gerstl's family; **64** (p. 121) © the copyright holder; **66** (p. 126) © the copyright holder; **69** (p. 129) © Estate of Dame Laura Knight. All rights reserved 2022/Bridgeman Images

British Library Cataloguing-in-Publication Data
A catalogue record for this book is available from the British Library

ISBN 978-1-3999-3150-2

Distributed outside the United States and Canada by ACC Art Books Ltd, Sandy Lane, Old Martlesham, Woodbridge, Suffolk IP12 4SD

Distributed in the United States and Canada by ARTBOOK | D.A.P., 75 Broad Street, Suite 630, New York, NY 10004

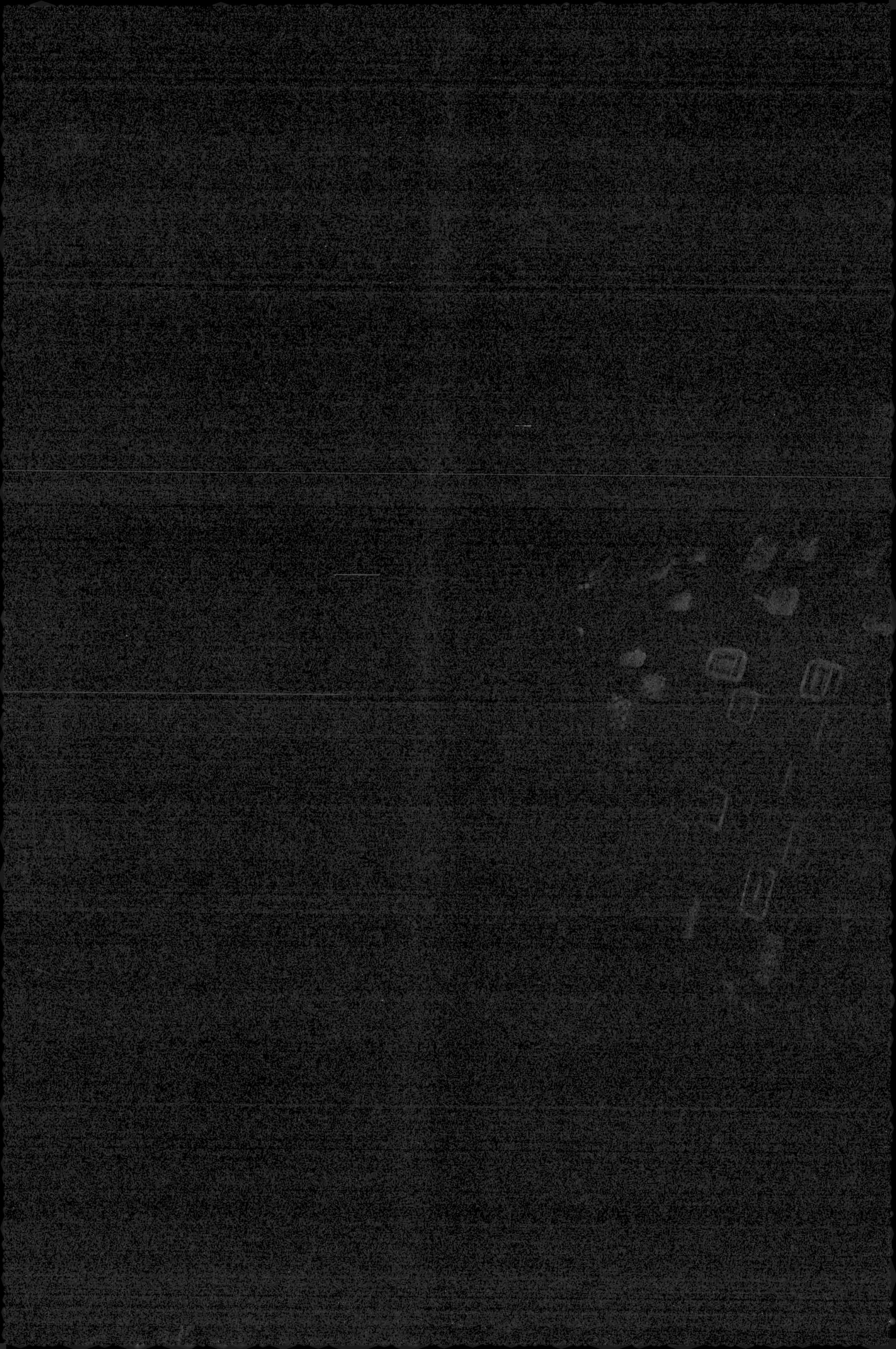